D0991942

CASTLES IN SPAIN
AND OTHER SCREEDS

THE WORKS OF
JOHN GALSWORTHY

NOVELS

VILLA RUBEIN: AND OTHER STORIES
THE ISLAND PHARISEES
THE MAN OF PROPERTY
THE COUNTRY HOUSE
FRATERNITY
THE PATRICIAN
THE DARK FLOWER
THE FREELANDS
BEYOND
FIVE TALES
SAINT'S PROGRESS
IN CHANCERY
TO LET
THE BURNING SPEAR
THE WHITE MONKEY
THE SILVER SPOON

THE FORSYTE SAGA

SHORT STORIES AND STUDIES

A COMMENTARY
A MOTLEY
THE INN OF TRANQUILLITY
THE LITTLE MAN
A SHEAF
ANOTHER SHEAF
TATTERDEMALION
CAPTURES
CASTLES IN SPAIN: AND OTHER SCREED

CARAVAN

VERSES NEW AND OLD

MEMORIES (ILLUSTRATED)
AWAKENING (ILLUSTRATED)
ADDRESSES IN AMERICA

PLAYS

FIRST SERIES:	THE SILVER BOX JOY STRIFE
SECOND SERIES:	THE ELDEST SON THE LITTLE DREAM JUSTICE
THIRD SERIES:	THE FUGITIVE THE PIGEON THE MOB
FOURTH SERIES:	A BIT O' LOVE FOUNDATIONS THE SKIN GAME
FIFTH SERIES:	A FAMILY MAN LOYALTIES WINDOWS
SIXTH SERIES:	THE FOREST OLD ENGLISH THE SHOW

The above Plays issued separately

SIX SHORT PLAYS:
THE FIRST AND THE LAST
THE LITTLE MAN
HALL-MARKED
DEFEAT
THE SUN
PUNCH AND GO

THE GROVE EDITION

The Novels, Stories, and Studies of John Galsworthy in small volumes

CASTLES IN SPAIN

AND OTHER SCREEDS

BY

JOHN GALSWORTHY

NEW YORK
CHARLES SCRIBNER'S SONS
1927

Printed in the United States of America

TO
ROSALIE NEISH

CONTENTS

CASTLES IN SPAIN

AN ADDRESS

CASTLES IN SPAIN

AN ADDRESS

OF what do we moderns dream? What are our castles in Spain?

This question crossed my mind in Seville cathedral, that stone fabric of man's greatest dream in the ages to which we have been accustomed to apply the word "dark." Travellers in Spain consulting their guide-books, read: "On the eighth day of July, in the year 1401, the Dean and Chapter of Seville assembled in the Court of the Elms and solemnly resolved: 'Let us build us a church so great that those who come after us may think us mad to have attempted it!' The church took one hundred and fifty years to build."

And in that glorious building, raised by five succeeding generations, one could not help wondering wherein lay the superiority of ourselves, Children of Light, over those old Sons of Darkness.

We too dream, no doubt—not always with a Freudian complex; and our dreams have results, such as the Great Dam at Assouan, the Roosevelt Dam in Arizona, the Woolworth Building, the Fourth Bridge, the Power Works at Niagara, the Panama Canal (which took one-tenth of the time the Sons of Darkness lavished on Seville cathedral). But all these things were dreamed and fabricked out for immediate material benefit. The old builders of pyramids, mosques and churches built for no physical advantage in this life. They carved and wrought and slowly lifted stone on stone for remote and, as they thought, spiritual ends. We moderns mine and forge and mason-up our monuments to the immediate profit of our bodies. Incidentally they may give pleasure to the spirit, but we did not exactly build them for that purpose. Have we raised anything really great in stone or brick for a mere idea since Christopher Wren built St. Paul's Cathedral?

Sons of Darkness and Children of Light, both have worshipped a half-truth. The ancients built for to-morrow in another world, forgetting that all of us have a to-day in this. They spent riches and labour to save the souls of their hierarchy, but they kept their labourers so poor that they had no souls to save. They left astounding testimony to human genius and tenacity, but it never seems to have ruffled their consciousness that they fashioned the beautiful with slavery, misery, and blood.

We moderns pursue what we call Progress. All our stupendous achievements have this progressive notion at their back. Brooklyn Bridge may look beautiful in any light, and Sheffield chimney-stacks may look beautiful in the dark, but they were not put up for that reason, nor even because we thought we were thereby handing our Presidents or Prime Ministers the keys of heaven. Modern engineers may be lovers of beauty and men of imagination, but their prime mistresses are Science, Industry, and Trade. We think that if we make the wheels go round fast enough mankind is bound to rise on the wings of wealth. Look after the body, we say, and the spirit will look after itself. Whether we save a greater proportion of our bodies than the ancients did of souls is the question; but no such trifling doubt shakes our belief in Progress. Our modern castle in Spain is in one word: "Production."

Most men and women have an instinctive love of beauty, and some natural pride in the work of their brains and hands: but machinery divides us from the ancients; quietly, gradually, it has shifted the central point of man's philosophy. Before the industrial era set in, men used to make things by hand; they were in some sort artists, with at least the craftsman's pride in their work. Now they press buttons, turn wheels; don't make completed articles; work with monotony at the section of an article—so many hours of machine-driving a day, the total result of which is never a man's individual achievement. "Intelligent specialism," says a writer on Labour Policy, "is one thing. It consists in one man learning how to do one thing specially well.

But the sort of specialising which consists in setting thousands of human beings during their whole working lives to such soul-destroying jobs as fixing the bristles into a hair-brush, pasting labels on jam-pots, or nearly any one of the varieties of machine-tending, is quite another thing. It is the utter negation of human nature."

The tendency of modern "Production" is to centre a man's interest not in his working day, but outside of it—at least, in the lower ranks of industry. The old artificers absorbed culture, such as it was, from their work. In these days culture, such as it is, is grafted on to the workman in his leisure, as antidote to wheel-driving. Hewers, delvers, drawers of water in the past never, perhaps, took interest in their work; and there are still many among us to-day to whom their work is of absorbing interest. But, on the whole, the change has put pride of quantity above pride of quality. In old days the good thing was often naturally supplied; nowadays it is more often artificially demanded.

No one objects to production sanely and coherently directed to fine purposes. But this Progress of ours, which is supposed to take care of our bodies, and of which machinery is the mistress—does it progress? We used to have the manor-house with half-a-dozen hovels in its support. Now we have twenty miles of handsome residences with a hundred and twenty miles of ugly back streets, reeking with smoke and redolent of dulness, dirt, and discontent. The proportions are still unchanged, and the purple patches of our great towns are too often as rouge on the cheeks and salve on the lips of a corpse. Is this really Progress?

True progress would mean levelling up and gradually extinguishing the disproportion between manor and hovel, residence and back street.

Let us fantastically conceive the civic authorities of London on the eighth day of July, in this year of grace, solemnly resolving: "We will remake of London a city so beautiful and sweet to dwell in, that those who come after us shall think us mad to have attempted it." It might well take five generations to remake of London a stainless city of Portland stone, full of baths and flowers and singing birds—not in cages. We should need a procession of civic authorities who steadily loved castles in Spain. For a civic body only lives about four years, and cannot bind its successor. I wonder if we have even begun to realise the difficulty of true progress in a democratic age? He who furnishes an antidote to the wasteful, shifting tendency of short immediate policies under a system of government by bodies elected for short terms might be the greatest benefactor of the age. For find that antidote we must, or discover democracy to be fraudulent.

Again, are we not unfortunate in letting civic life be run by those who were born seeing two inches before their noses, and whose education, instead of increasing, has reduced those inches to one? It seems ungrateful to criticise the practical business man, whose stamina and energy make the more imaginative gasp. One owes him much, but one would like to owe him more. For does his vision as a rule extend beyond keeping pace with the present? And without vision—the people perish! Has not the word "visionary" come to have a slighting significance? And yet, unless we incorporate beauty in our scheme of life to-day, and teach the love of beauty to our children, the life of to-morrow and the children thereof must needs be as far from beauty as we are now. Isn't it, then, peculiar to set men to direct the education, housing, and amusements of their fellow-citizens, unless they have a love of beauty and some considerable knowledge of art? And have not the present generation of business men —with notable exceptions—a sort of indulgent contempt for art and beauty? A few years ago the Headmaster of a great Public School made use of these words: "I'm glad to see so many boys going in for art; it is an excellent hobby to pass the time *when you have nothing better to do?*" He had been teaching Greek for half a century; yet it was Greek to him that art has been the greatest factor in raising mankind from its old savage state. The contemplation of beautiful visions, emotions, thoughts, and dreams, expressed beautifully in words, stone, metal, paint, and music, has slowly, generation by generation, uplifted man and mollified his taste for "long pig"—as the South Sea Islander calls his edible enemy. Even the uplifting part of religion is but the beautiful expression of exalted feeling. The rest of religion (including the ceremony of eating "long pig") is only superstition. Think of the thousand wars fought in the name of superstition; the human sacrifices, the tortures of the Inquisition; the persecutions, intolerances, and narrow cruelties perpetrated even to this day! The teachings of Buddha, of Christ, of St. Francis d'Assisi were the expression of exalted feeling; simple, and touching the hearts of men, as all true beauty does. They have done an ennobling work. But who shall deny that they belong to the cult of beauty?

Trade—they say—has been a mollifying

factor, an elevator in the human hotel. Yes, in so far as it opens up communications, and is the coach in which art and beauty ride; but *of itself*—it has no elevating influence.

Beauty, alone, in the largest sense of the word—the yearning for it, the contemplation of it—has civilised mankind. And no human being ever contributed to that process who thought he had "something better to do." And yet, we don't take beauty seriously. Immediate profit rules the roost in this Age of ours, and I leave it to the conscience of the Age to decide whether that is good. For every Age has a conscience; though it never comes to life till the Age is on its death-bed.

The fault of all Ages, perhaps, has been that the knowledge and the love of beauty should have been kept as a preserve for the few, the possession of a caste or clique. No great proportion of us are capable of creating or expressing beauty; but an immensely greater proportion of us are capable of appreciating it than have ever been given the chance of so doing. It should be our castle in Spain to clear our Age of that defect, and put beauty within the reach of all.

Machinery, of course, has come to stay; and though it may be true that engineers, authors, stone-cutters, artists, and many others still love beauty and take pride in their work, the great majority of us—label-pasters, wheel-drivers, stokers, clerks, shop-girls, bristle-fixers—are the slaves of modern machinery. For all such we must rely on grafted culture now; in other words, on education, rousing and fostering in the young that instinct for beauty which is in nearly all of us. For this, we have exceptional facilities nowadays. Besides teaching cooking and the fine art of being clean, we can bring an inkling of the other fine arts, architecture, literature, painting, music, of past and present, to children even in the humblest schools; we can teach children to appreciate the beauty of Nature, and give them some idea of taste. Revolution or evolution—we glibly talk of now one, now the other, but both are vain unless they mean demand for greater dignity of human life. What use in B despoiling A if B is going to use his spoils no better, perhaps worse, than A?

The word beauty is not here used in any precious sense. Its precious definitions are without number, or—value to speak of. No! It is here used to mean everything which promotes the true dignity of human life. For instance, to be "a good sport"—as they say—a man will shun that which lowers his dignity, dims his idea of his own quality; and his conception of his own quality derives obscurely from his sense of beauty. The dignity of human life demands, in fact, not only such desirable embroideries as pleasant sound, fine form, and lovely colour, but health, strength, cleanliness, balance, joy in living, just conduct and kind conduct. A man who truly loves beauty hates to think that he enjoys it at the expense of starved and stunted human beings or suffering animals. Mere æstheticism can be cruel or pettifogging; but such is not the beauty which gleams on the heights in the sunrise—certainly not our castle in Spain.

Sentiment apart, the ideal of beauty is the best investment modern man can make; for nothing else—not even trade—will keep him from extirpating the human species. Science in the hands of engineers and chemists has developed destructive powers which increase a hundredfold with each decade, while the reproductive powers and inclinations of the human being do not vary. Nothing in the world but the love of beauty in its broad sense stands between Man and the full and reckless exercise of his competitive appetites. The Great War was a little war compared with that which, through the development of scientific destruction, might be waged next time. There is, then, sheer necessity for investment in the ideal of beauty. No other security will give us interest on our money, and our money back. Unbalanced trade, science, industry give, indeed, a high momentary rate of interest, but only till the crash comes again and the world goes even more bankrupt than it is at present. The professor who invented a rocket which would visit the moon, find out all about it, and come back with the story, would have done more real good if he had taught a school full of children to see the beauty of—moonshine.

The next war will be fought from the air, and from under the sea, with explosives, gas, and the germs of disease. It may be over before it is declared. The final war necessary for the complete extirpation of mankind will be fought, perhaps, with atomic energy; and we shall have no occasion to examine the moon, for the earth will be as lifeless.

But it is sentiment which really makes the wheels go round, for not even "big business" rules our instincts and passions, and the question for modern man is: What shall we be sentimental about? Which is the fairer castle in Spain—quantity or quality—blind production or the dignity of human life?

What ideals have we at present? Happiness in a future life. If there be a future life for the individual, shall we find it repaying if we have not striven for quality in this; not had that kind and free and generous philosophy which belongs to the cult of beauty, and alone gives peace of mind? The pursuit of beauty includes, then, whatever may be true in the ideal of happiness in a future life. We have another current ideal: wealth or comfort in this life. But the cult of beauty contains all that is good in that; for it demands physical health and well-being, sane minds in sane bodies, which depend on a sufficiency of material comfort. The rest of the ideal of wealth is mere fat, sagging beyond the point of balance. Modern civilisation offers us, in fact, a compound between "happiness in a future life" and "material comfort in this," lip-serving the first, and stomach-serving the second. You get the keys of heaven from your bank, but not unless you have a good balance. Modern civilisation, on the whole, is camouflaged commercialism, wherein to do things well for the joy of doing them well is mere eccentricity. We even commercialise salvation—for so much virtue, so much salvation! *Quid pro quo!*

To give the devil its due, ours is the best Age men ever lived in; we are all more comfortable and virtuous than we ever were; we have many new accomplishments, advertisements in green pastures, telephones in bedrooms, more newspapers than we want to read, and extremely punctilious diagnosis of maladies. A doctor examined a young lady the other day, and among his notes were these: "Not afraid of small rooms, ghosts, or thunderstorms—not made drunk by hearing Wagner; brown hair, artistic hands; had a craving for chocolate in 1918." The Age is most thorough and accomplished, but with a kind of deadly practicality. All for to-day, nothing for to-morrow! The future will never think us mad for attempting what we do attempt; we build no Seville cathedrals. We never get ahead of time. For instance, we have just let slip a chance to revitalise the country life of England. At demobilisation we might have put hundreds of thousands on the land, which needs them so very badly. And we have put in all not so many as the war took off the land. Life on the land means hard work and few cinemas; but it also means hearty stock for the next generation, and the power of feeding ourselves on an island which the next war might completely isolate. A nation which never looks ahead is in for rude awakenings.

The pursuit of beauty as a national ideal, the building of that castle in Spain, requires, of course, foresight, long and patient labour, and steadfastness of ideal.

All literary men can tell people what they ought not to be; that is—literature. But to tell them what they ought to do is—politics, and it would be mere impertinence for a literary man to suggest anything practical!

But let him, at least, make a few affirmations. He believes that modern man is a little further from being a mere animal than the men of the Dark Ages, however great the castles in Spain those men left for us to look upon; but he is sure that we are in far greater danger than ever they were of a swift decline. From that decline he is convinced that only the love and cult of beauty will save us.

By the love and cult of beauty he means: *a higher and wider conception of the dignity of human life;* the teaching of what beauty is, to all—not merely to the few; the cultivation of good-will, so that we wish and work and dream that not only ourselves but everybody may be healthy and happy; and, above all, the fostering of the habit of doing things and making things well, for the joy of the work and the pleasure of achievement, rather than for the gain they will bring us. With these as the rules, instead of, as now, the riders, the wheels of an insensate scientific industrialism, whose one idea is to make money and get ahead of other people, careless of direction toward heaven or hell, might conceivably be spoked. Our Age lacks an ideal expressed with sufficient concreteness to be like a vision beckoning. In these unsuperstitious days no other ideal seems worthy of us, or indeed possible to us, save beauty—or call it, if you will, the dignity of human life.

Writers sometimes urge the need for more spiritual beauty in our lives. I distrust the word spiritual. We must be able to smell, and see, hear, feel, and taste our ideal as well; must know by plain evidence that it is lifting human life, the heritage of all, not merely of the refined and leisured. The body and soul are one for the purpose of all real evolution, and regrettable is any term suggestive of divorce between them. The dignity of human life is an unmistakable and comprehensive phrase. Offence against it is the modern Satan. We can say "Retro, Satanas," by leaving, each of us, a tiny corner of the universe a little more dignified, lovely, and lovable than we found it.

Latest opinion—unless there is a later—assigns ten thousand years as the time during which what we know as civilisation has been at work. But ten thousand years is a considerable period of mollification, and one had rashly hoped that traditions of gentleness and fair-play had more strength among Western peoples than they have been proved to have since 1914; that mob feeling might have been less, instead of, as it seems, more potent. And yet, alongside of stupidity, savagery, greed, and mob violence, run an amazing individual patience, good humour, endurance, and heroism, which save a man from turning his back on himself and the world, with the words: "Cats and monkeys, monkeys and cats; all life is there!" Fear, after all, is at the back of nearly all savagery; and man must infallibly succumb to the infections of fear if there be not present in him that potent antidote—the sense of human dignity, which is but a love of and a belief in beauty. What applies to the individual applies to the civilisation of which he forms a part. Our civilisation, if it is to endure, must have a star on which to fix its eyes—something distant and magnetic to draw it on, something to strive towards, beyond the troubled and shifting needs and passions and prejudices of the moment. Those who wish to raise the dignity of human life should try to give civilisation that star, to equip the world with the only vision which can save it from spite and the crazy competitions which lead thereto. The past few years have been the result of the past few hundred years. The war was no spasmodic visitation, but the culmination of age-long competitions. The past few years have devoured many millions of grown men, more millions of little children—prevented their birth, killed them, or withered them for life. If modern individuals and modern nations pursue again these crazy competitions, without regard for the dignity of human life, we shall live to see ten millions perish for every million who perished in this war. We shall live to curse the day, when, at the end of so great a lesson, we were too practical and business-like to take it to heart.

Facts must be faced, and ideals should be grounded in reality; for it is no use blinking the general nature of man, or thinking that Rome can be built in a day. But with all our prejudices and passions, and all our "business instinct," we have also the instinct for beauty, and a sense of what is dignified. On that we must build, if we wish to leave to those who come after us the foundations of a castle in Spain such as the world has not yet seen; to leave our successors in mood and heart to continue our work, so that one hundred and fifty years, perhaps, from now human life may really be dignified and beautiful, not just a breathless, grudging, visionless scramble from birth to death, of a night with no star alight.

1920.

WHERE WE STAND

WHERE WE STAND

CIVILISATION? Is it learned and wealthy social organisation? Or is it general gentility? Without agreeing on any ethical definition we may admit that the most civilised state will be that wherein is found the greatest proportionate number of happy, healthy, wise, and gentle citizens. Whether civilisation, judged by this standard, has ever been high, is more than doubtful; it was certainly still low before the war, and is at the moment even lower. The Great War was not a thunderbolt from the blue launched at an unoffending mankind: it was a stealing Fate carefully nurtured within the bosom of modern civilisation; the natural and gradually reached result of a crude competitive system pursued almost to its limits—the climax, in fact, of the individual, political, and national rivalries which have been speeding to this end since the Middle Ages.

The march of mankind is directed neither by his will, nor by his superstitions, but by the effect of his great and, as it were, accidental discoveries on his average nature. The discovery and exploitation of language, of fire, of corn, of ships, of metals, of gunpowder, of printing, of coal, steam, electricity, of flying machines (atomic energy has still to be exploited), acting on a human nature which is, practically speaking, constant, moulds the real shape of human life, under all the agreeable camouflage of religions, principles, policies, personages, and ideas. After the discovery and exploitation of gunpowder and printing, the centuries stood somewhat still, until, with coal, steam, and modern machinery, a swift industrialism set in, which has brought the world to its recent state.

In comparison with the effect of these discoveries and their unconscious influence on human life, the effect of political ideas is seen to be inconsiderable. For theories arise from and follow material states of being, rather than precede and cause them. British Liberalism, for example, did not give birth to that hard-headed child Free Trade (by Wealth out of Short Sight); it did not even inaugurate the "live and let live" theory; it followed on and crowned with a misty halo a state of long-acknowledged industrial ascendancy. Prussian "will to power" did not cause, it followed and crowned with thorns, the rising wave of German industry and wealth. And outstanding personalities such as Gladstone and Bismarck are rather made outstanding by the times they live in, than make those times outstanding.

This is one of two sober truths with which one has to reckon in forecasting the future of civilisation; the other is the aforesaid constancy of human nature. The fact that modern human nature is much more subtle, ambitious, and humane than the nature of primitive man, is not greatly important to creatures who live but three-score years and ten, and who in their mental and spiritual stature are on the whole no higher, and in physical development probably lower, than the Greeks and Romans.

A cataclysm such as this war makes

stock-takers of us all; and we are now recording in a hundred ways, with a sort of automatic busyness, where we stand, with the praiseworthy intention, no doubt, of standing somewhere else. We shall point out to ourselves where we failed, and what we have now to do, and probably proceed to do what our inventions and discoveries, acting on our general nature, make us. This fatalistic reflection, however, should incite us to effort, rather than discourage us therefrom; for it is no use labouring under illusions; mankind, which does not see the grip his discoveries have on him, is the more powerless against that grip. Nor is there any use in being blind about the sort of beings we are. Consider for a moment that queer compound, average human nature. Plain every-day man, superior to his exploiters, pastors, and masters, in the qualities of hardihood, endurance, patience, and humour, is inferior to them in power of imagining, speculating, devising, competing, and telling others what to do. The competitive and scheming qualities of these leaders—of politicians, militarists, industrial captains and exploiters, of pressmen, labour leaders, lawyers, pastors, and writers—form, with the simple qualities of those they lead, that amalgam which we call average human nature. But leaders and led are almost equally deficient in pure altruism—the impersonal quality; so that, in sum, human nature is personal, strenuous, hardy, enduring, ingenious, short-sighted, combative, and competitive—just the right material to be stampeded by its own discoveries and inventions.

The war has not changed human nature by jot or tittle, and has added to, rather than taken from, our undigested inventions and discoveries: it has, for instance, developed engines of destruction, and flying machines, whether for purposes of trade or war, and increased general ingenuity and the possibilities of material production. What else has it done? It has carted the hay of old national boundaries and problems, and produced a luxuriant crop of fresh ones. It has destroyed some autocracies and created others which threaten fresh tyrannies of the part over the whole. It has revolutionised Russia, probably forever; it has wasted the youth and wealth of Europe to such a degree as to shift the real storm-centre of the world to the Pacific Ocean and the three unexhausted countries lying east and west thereof. It has exaggerated the conception of nationalism and, on the whole, lowered that of individual liberty.

It has brought forth the theory of a league of nations, which will, alas, remain a beneficent theory unless, to their own uneasy surprise, the now dominant powers should suddenly become more altruistic. It has greatly advanced the emancipation of women, and loosened family life. It has increased the hopes and wants of "the workers"—a name which suggests a monopoly by no means existing. It has, by development of flying, turned both land-warfare and sea-power into gambles in the air. It has demonstrated the need for nations to be self-sufficing in the matter of food-growth, without inspiring, apparently, in this English land any intention of so becoming. It has not, so far as one can see, altered in the least the only accepted ideal of modern states—maximum production of wealth to the square mile.

Now the sole hope that the future of civilisation may be better than its past or present centres round the possibility of substituting for that bankrupt ideal the ideal of the maximum production of health and happiness; for, whatever the fashion of our talk and the complexion of our thought, this is not precisely the same thing. To judge from the speeches of some of their leaders, the "workers," indeed, would seem to be feeling after such a substitution. But it may well be doubted whether many of their followers have risen to more than a partisan conception of the need, or fathomed the roots of the evil.

For an example by the way: There is going on in this country a great hubbub concerning coal-production, nationalisation of mines, and so forth. Only a wildered pelican here and there croaks of the need to concentrate national attention on chaining the tides and using water-driven electricity, on opening up oil-deposits, or converting coal into oil. Coal is a curse, if there is any way of doing without it. For, with all its usefulness, its smoke has done more to destroy health and happiness than any of our great discoveries. And, even if it were rendered smokeless, it has still to be extracted, and millions of men in this beautiful world must work below ground. We are told, with clamour, that on coal-production our exporting power depends—power to pay for the food we now have to import. Only in apologetic whispers are we told that we should grow the food instead—which is possible in far greater degree than at present—and save that amount of need for coal. And why this fatalistic attitude about coal? Simply because we are still in the rut made by an exploited discovery acting on average human nature: we know that we have huge unextracted stores of coal; many of us own coal-mines or shares therein; more of us make a living by extracting coal: our rulers depend on the votes of a coal-worshipping community; *we want wealth quickly;* in sum, we are human beings and prefer each of us his own immediate profit to what will benefit us all in the future. That is a short concrete example of why the future of civilisation looks black.

We are all borne along in the car of industry, driven by that blind driver, our own competitive mood. What applies to ourselves applies to other nations. America and Japan are going our way fast, becoming town-ridden, industry-mad communities. The next great war will probably begin between them. Even the Chinese are now infected by the Western idea of maximum wealth to the square mile. Their "advanced" men are saying, "We must adopt Western methods or we cannot compete with Western industry." Pursue Industrialism without the two basic safeguards—self-growth of food by every nation, and the diversion of the spirit of competition to things of the mind, to art, and to sport and adventure—pursue it thus unguarded, and civilisation cannot hope to advance. Proceed as the nations may with plans for economy, for housing, sanitation, education, industrial expansion, a hundred other things, they cannot keep pace with the ruin implicit in their progress, while their ideal remains, just crudely, maximum production of wealth to the square mile.

Nations, like men, can be healthy and happy, though comparatively poor. Better, if need be, limit population scientifically, than go on scuttling and scuffling down this road of danger. Wealth is a means to an end, not the end itself. As a synonym for health and happiness, it has had fair trial, has failed dismally, and brought on us this war.

Remembering that human nature remains the same, that inventions are always with us, and that men almost invariably learn by experience too late—*si jeunesse savait, si vieillesse pouvait*—civilisation appears to be in an *impasse*. When we are assured by statesmen that the bad old world must and shall pass away, we naturally ask ourselves why—failing any real change of directing mood—it should become anything but worse. Must we, then, throw up our hands and say, "Well, we're only human beings: we do what we can, and after all, in some respects the world is better than it was, even if we *are* heading for a conflagration more hideous than the last?" Or is there any way in which we can try to struggle up out of the *impasse?*

If there be a saving way, at all, it is obviously this: Substitute health and happiness for wealth as a world-ideal; and translate that new ideal into action by *education* from babyhood up. To do this, States must reorganise the spirit of education—in other words, must introduce religion; not the old formal creeds, but the humanistic religion of service for the common weal, the religion of a social honour which puts the health and happiness of all first and the wealth of self second.

The only comfort in the situation is the curious fact that, underneath all else, the sociability inculcated in modern nations by quick communications and incessant intercourse is already tending toward the formation of this new humanistic religion. But at present the tendency lacks proper machinery for expression of itself. The main object of education now is material advancement, with some honourable hankering after spiritual training. It should be the other way round. Boys and girls should be taught to think first of others in material things; they should be infected with the wisdom to know that in making smooth the way of all lies the road to their own health and happiness. It is a question of the *mood* in which we are taught to learn. That mood, from school-age up, should be shaped so as to correct, and not, as at present, to emphasise our natural competitive egoism. None can do this save teachers themselves inspired by this ideal of service for the common welfare. The first need of civilisation, therefore, is the finding and equipping of such teachers.

The teaching profession should be honoured before all others; the direction of its ideals, standards, and curricula, the choice of its man-power and woman-power placed in the hands of the most truly enlightened and sweet-living persons in the State—not mere capable administrators or scholars, but men and women who have shown in practice that they can rise to an altruistic conception of human existence. States should spend money and effort as freely on this great all-underlying matter of right education as they have hitherto spent them on beating and destroying each other.

Economic production, science, development, and discovery cannot save us, pursued in the rampant competitive mood. Trade is not a good in itself, fostering as it must the sharp and selfishly competitive qualities. Instead of the trading mood, we need a sort of universal sportsmanship, the basis of a mood which, competing keenly in things of the spirit—in architecture, art, music, letters, and such science as ministers to health and happiness—competing, too, in sports and in adventure, agrees to pool all productive and industrial endeavour, and to put the material welfare of mankind first, and the material welfare of self second; and we need that such a mood should be beyond and above all narrow national prejudice and partisanship.

The real and supreme importance of the League of Nations consists in its power of giving such a mood the first chance it has ever had in international affairs. For it must freely be confessed that, without this chance in international affairs, there is no hope that the mood will be adopted and fostered nationally.

Failing then the success of the League of Nations in leading to the general establishment of this new mood governing our lives, civilisation will continue to advance only in the public press and the mouths of statesmen in all countries, deeply, if unconsciously, committed to the devil. Nay, it must steadily lead us to another world-catastrophe many times worse than that we have just encountered, because of our blind progress in the use of destructive mechanism. In that event those of us who are left alive will console ourselves with the thought that we are human beings—of whom too much cannot be expected.

1920.

INTERNATIONAL THOUGHT

INTERNATIONAL THOUGHT

"The exchange of international thought is the only possible salvation of the world."

TO those who, until 1914, believed in civil behaviour between man and man, the war and its ensuing peace brought disenchantment. Preoccupied with the humaner pursuits, and generally unfamiliar with the real struggle for existence, they were caught napping. The rest of mankind have experienced no particular astonishment—the doing-down of man by man was part of daily life, and when it was done collectively they felt no spiritual change. It was dreadful and—natural. This may not be a popular view of human life in the mass, but it is true. Average life is a long fight; this man's success is that man's failure; co-operation and justice are only the palliatives of a basic, and ruthless, competition. The disenchantment of the few would not have mattered so much but for the fact that they were the nerves and voice of the community. Their histories, poems, novels, plays, pictures, treatises, sermons were the expression of what we call civilisation. And disenchanted philosophers, though by so much the nearer to the truths of existence, are by that much, perhaps, the less useful to human nature. We need scant reminder of a truth always with us, we need rather perpetual assertion that the truth might with advantage be, and may possibly with effort become, less unpleasant. Though we ought to look things in the face, afflatus is the essence of ethical philosophy.

It is a pity, then, that philosophy is, or has been, draggle-tailing—art avoiding life, taking to contraptions of form and colour signifying nothing; literature driven in on itself, or running riot; science more hopeful of perfecting poison gas than of abating coal-smoke or curing cancer; that religion should incline to tuck its head under the wing of spiritualism; that there should be, in fact, a kind of tacit abandonment of the belief in life. Sport, which still keeps a flag of idealism flying, is perhaps the most saving grace in the world at the moment, with its spirit of rules kept, and regard for the adversary, whether the fight is going for or against. When, if ever, the fair-play spirit of sport reigns over international affairs, the cat force which rules there now will slink away and human life emerge for the first time from jungle.

Looking the world in the face, we see what may be called a precious mess. Under a thin veneer—sometimes no veneer—of regard for civilisation, each country, great and small, is pursuing its own ends, struggling to rebuild its own house in the burnt village. The dread of confusion-worse-confounded, of death re-crowned, and pestilence revivified alone keeps the nations to the compromise of peace. What chance has a better spirit?

"The exchange of international thought is the only possible salvation of the world" are the words of Thomas Hardy, and so true that it may be well to cast an eye over such mediums as we have for the exchange of international thought. "The Permanent Court of International Justice"; "The League of Nations"; "The Pan-American Congress"; certain sectional associations of this nation with that nation, tarred somewhat with the brush of self-interest; sporadic international conferences concerned with sectional interests; and such societies as the Rotary International, the International Confederation of Students, and the P.E.N. Club, an international association of writers with friendly aims, but no political intentions. These are about all, and they are taken none too seriously by the peoples of the earth. The salvation of a world in which we all live, however, would seem to have a certain importance. Why, then, is not more attention paid to the only existing means of salvation? The argument for neglect is much as follows: Force has always ruled human life—it always will. Competition is basic. Co-operation and justice succeed, indeed, in definite communities so far as to minimise the grosser forms of crime, but only because general opinion within the ring-fence of a definite community gives them an underlying force which the individual offender cannot withstand. There is no such ring-fence round nations, therefore no general opinion, and no underlying force to ensure the abstention of individual nations from crime—if, indeed, transgression of laws which are not fixed can be called crime.

This is the average hard-headed view at the moment. If it is to remain dominant, there is no salvation in store for the world. "Why not?" replied the hard-head. "It always has been the view, and the world has gone on?" True! But the last few years have brought a startling change in the conditions of existence—a change which has not yet been fully realised. *Destructive science has gone ahead out of all proportion.* It is developing so fast that each irresponsible assertion of national rights or interests brings the world appreciably nearer to ruin. Without any doubt whatever the powers of destruction are gaining fast on the powers of creation and construction. In old days a thirty years' war was needed to exhaust a nation; it will soon be (if it is not already) possible to exhaust a nation in a week by the destruction of its big towns from the air. The conquest of the air, so jubilantly hailed by the unthinking, may turn out the most sinister event that ever befell us, simply because it came before we were fit for it—fit to act reasonably under the temptation of its fearful possibilities. The use made of it in the last war showed that; and the sheep-like refusal of the startled nations to face the new situation, and unanimously ban chemical warfare and the use of flying for destructive purposes, shows it still more clearly. No one denies that the conquest of the air was a great, a wonderful achievement; no one denies that it could be a beneficent achievement if the nations would let it be. But mankind has not yet, apparently, reached a pitch of decency sufficient to be trusted with such an inviting and terribly destructive weapon. We are all familiar with the argument: Make war dreadful enough, and there will be no war. And we none of us believe in it. The last war disproved it utterly. Competition in armaments has already begun, among men who think, to mean competition in the air. Nothing else will count in a few years' time. We have made through our science a monster that will devour us yet unless by exchanging international thought we can create a general opinion against the new powers of destruction so strong and so unanimous that no nation will care to face the force which underlies it.

A well-known advocate of the League of Nations said the other day: "I do not believe it necessary that the League should have a definite force at its disposal. It could not maintain a force that would keep any first-rate power from breaking the peace. Its strength lies in the use of publicity; in its being able to voice universal disapproval with all the latent potentiality of universal action."

Certainly, the genuine publication of all military movements and developments throughout the world, the unfathoming and broadcasting of destructive inventions and devices, would bring us nearer to salvation than any covenant can do. If the world's chemists and the world's engineers would hold annual meetings in a friendly spirit for the salvation of mankind! If they could agree together that to exercise their ingenuity on the perfecting of destructive agents for the use of governments was a crime; to take money for it a betrayal of their species! If we could have such exchange of international thought as that, then indeed we might hear the rustle of salvation's wings. And—after all—why not? The answer to the question—Is there to be happiness or misery, growth or ruin for the human species?—does not now lie with governments. Governments are competitive trustees for competitive sections of mankind. Put destruction in their hands and they will use it to further the interests of those for whom they are trustees; just as they will use and even inspire the spiritual poison gas of pressmen. The real key to the future is in the hands of those who provide the means of destruction. Are scientists (chemists, inventors, engineers) to be Americans, Englishmen, Frenchmen, Germans, Japanese, Russians, before they are men, in this matter of the making of destruction? Are they to be more concerned with the interests of their own countries, or with the interests of the human species? That has become the question they have to answer now that they have for the first time the future of the human race within their grasp. Modern invention has taken such a vast stride forward that the incidence of responsibility is changed. It rests on Science as it never did before; on Science, and on—Finance. There again the exchange of international thought has become terrifically important. The financiers of the world, for instance, in the light of their knowledge, under the pressure of their difficulties, out of the motive of mutual aid, could certainly devise some real and lasting economic betterment, if only they would set to work steadily, not spasmodically, to exchange international thought.

Hard-head's answer to such suggestions

is: "Nonsense! Inventors, chemists, engineers, financiers, all have to make their living, and are just as disposed to believe in their own countries as other men. Their pockets and the countries who guarantee those pockets have first call on them." Well! That has become the point. If neither Science nor Finance will agree to think internationally, there is probably nothing for it but to kennel-up in disenchantment, and wait for an end which can't be very long in coming—not a complete end, of course, say a general condition of affairs similar to that which existed recently in the famine provinces of Russia.

It is easy to be pessimistic, and easy to indulge in cheap optimism; to steer between the two is hard. We still have a chance of saving and improving such civilisation as we have; but this chance depends on how far we succeed in exchanging international thought in the next few years. To some the word international has a socialistic, even communistic significance. But, as here used, it has nothing whatever to do with economic theories, class divisions, or political aims. The exchange of international thought, which alone can save us, is the exchange of thought between *craftsmen*—between the statesmen of the different countries, the lawyers of the different countries; the scientists, the financiers, the writers of the different countries. We have the mediums of exchange (however inadequately made use of) for the statesmen and the lawyers, but the scientists (inventors, chemists, engineers) and the financiers, the two sets of craftsmen in whose hands the future of the world chiefly lies, at present lack adequate machinery for the exchange of international thought, and adequate conception of the extent to which world responsibility now falls on them. If they could once realise the supreme nature of that responsibility, the battle of salvation should be half won.

Coming to the exchange of international thought in one's own craft, there seem three ways in which writers, as such, can help to ease the future of the world. They can be friendly and hospitable to the writers of other countries—and for this purpose exists the international P.E.N. Club, with its many and increasing branches. They can recognise and maintain the principle that works of the imagination, indeed all works of art, are the property of mankind at large, and not merely of the country of their origin; that to discontinue (for example) during a war with Germany the reading of German poetry, the listening to German music, the looking at German pictures, was a harmful absurdity which should never be repeated. Any real work of art, individual and racial though it be in root and fibre, is impersonal and universal in its appeal. Art is one of the great natural links (perhaps the only great natural link) between the various breeds of men, and to scotch its gentling influence in time of war is to confess ourselves still apes and tigers. Only writers can spread this creed, only writers can keep the door open for art during national feuds; and it is their plain duty to do this service to mankind

The third and greatest way in which the writer can ease the future is simply stated in the words: Fair Play. The power of the Press is a good third to the powers of Science and Finance. If the Press, as a whole, never diverged from fair report; if it refused to give unmeasured service to party or patriotic passion; if it played the game as Sport plays it—what a clearance of the air! At present, with, of course, many and distinguished exceptions, the Press in every country plays the game according to rules of its own which have too little acquaintance with those of Sport.

The Press is manned by a great crew of writers, the vast majority of whom have in private life a higher standard of fair play than that followed by the Press ship they man. They would, I believe, be the first to confess that. Improvement in Press standards of international and political fair play can only come from the individual writers who make up the Press. And such reform will not come until editors and journalists acquire the habit of exchanging thought internationally, of broadening their minds and hearts with other points of view, of recognising that they must treat as they would themselves be treated. Only, in short, when they do as they would, most of them, individually choose to do, will a sort of word-miasma cease to breed international agues and fever. We do not commonly hold in private life that ends justify means. Why should they be held to justify means in Press life—why should report so often be accepted without due examination when it is favourable to one's views, rejected without due examination when it is unfavourable? why should the other side's view be burked so often? and so on, and so on. The Press has great power and professes high ideals; it has much virtue; it does great service; but it does greater harm when, for whatever reason, it diverges from truth, or from the principles of fair play.

To sum up, Governments and Peoples are no longer in charge. Our fate is really in the hands of the three great Powers—Science, Finance, and the Press. Underneath the showy political surface of things, those three great Powers are secretly determining the march of the nations; and there is little hope for the future unless they can mellow and develop on international lines. In each of these departments of life there must be men who feel this as strongly as the writer of these words. The world's hope lies with them; in the possibility of their being able to institute a sort of craftsman's trusteeship for mankind—a new triple alliance, of Science, Finance, and the Press, in service to a new idealism. Nations, in block, will never join hands, never have much in common, never be able to see each other's points of view. The outstanding craftsmen of the nations have a far better chance of seeing eye to eye; they have the common ground of their craft, and a livelier vision. What divides them at present is a too narrow sense of patriotism, and—to speak crudely—money. Inventors must exist; financiers live; and papers pay. And, here, Irony smiles. Though Science, Finance, and the Press at present seem to doubt it, there is, still, more money to be made out of the salvation of mankind than out of its destruction; a better and more enduring livelihood for these three Estates. And yet without the free exchange of international thought we may be fairly certain that the present purely national basis of their livelihoods will persist, and if it does the human race will not, or at least so meagrely that it will be true to say of it, as of Anatole France's old woman: "It lives—but so little!"

1923.

ON EXPRESSION

AN ADDRESS

ON EXPRESSION *

AN ADDRESS

EXPRESSION is my subject; and no mariner embarking on the endless waters of the Atlantic in a Canadian canoe could feel more lost than the speaker who ventures on a theme so wide and inexhaustible. And yet—how pleasant to know that it doesn't matter how one steers; for in no case can one arrive! The barque of discourse must needs be lifted every which way, veer helplessly in the winds and cross-currents of the measureless, and trace a crazy line.

Let me hazard, however, a prefatory axiom, about expression as a whole: The soul of good expression is an unexpectedness which, still, keeps to the mark of meaning, and does not betray truth. Fresh angles, new lights; but neither at the expense of

* Presidential Address to the English Association, 1924.

significance, nor to the detriment of verity; never, in fact, just for the sake of being unexpected.

Following first the incorrigible bent of a novelist, let me proffer a speculation or two on the connexion between expression and character-drawing. Hardly any figures in prose fiction seem to survive the rust of Time unless burnished by happy extravagance, saved by a tinge of irony, or inhabited by what one may call "familiar spirit." The creations of such writers as Rabelais, Cervantes, Dumas, and Dickens may serve to illustrate survival through happy extravagance; of Fielding, Jane Austen, Thackeray, and Anatole France through ironical tincture; of Tolstoy through "familiar spirit."

We all understand happy extravagance, however incapable of it we may be; nor do we find any great difficulty in appreciating the preservative qualities of an ironic humour, which is very much a part of English character. I need not, then, dwell on expression in regard to these. "Familiar spirit" is a more mysterious affair. The characters in fictions who are inhabited by "familiar spirit" are such as convince the reader that he might meet and recognise them walking the every-day world. Mr. Hardy's "Tess," Mr. Moore's "Esther," Mr. Bennett's "Elsie" in *Riceyman Steps,* and Mr. Wells's "Kipps" are good English specimens of character so endowed. But one may gather more easily from Tolstoy's creations in *War and Peace* and *Anna Karenin,* than from any English examples, the nature of this quality. It demands an unself-consciousness rare in English and French novelists—perfectly simple expression, without trick, manner, or suspicion of desire to seem clever, modern, æsthetic. Tolstoy was lost, indeed, in the creative mood when he made "Natasha," "Pierre," and "Anna."

"Familiar spirit," however, may inhabit a whole book and ensure its permanence, although that book contains no characters who remain in the mind: *Cranford, The Golden Age, The Purple Land* occur to me as instances. And probably the perfect example of "familiar spirit" permeating both book and its characters is Mark Twain's *Huckleberry Finn*—that joyous work as sure of immortality as any book I know. While on the question of resistance to Time, we ought, I suppose, to be wondering how much longer bulk is going to count in the equation of survival. Life driven by inventions from pillar to post has ever less time in its bank for us to draw on. But the persistent popularity of *Don Quixote, Tom Jones, David Copperfield, War and Peace,* and other very long masterpieces seems to contradict the logical suspicion that economy of expression must favour durability. The contemporary novel, at all events, shows, little sign of shrinkage. Expression seems rather to be taking the bit between its teeth, and galloping on the road. Ours is an experimental epoch. New doctrines obtain. It has become, for instance, something of a fashion to feel that under the fevering influence of emotional stress we are all alike. Hero—they say—differs little from hero, when both are in pursuit of heroines. Villains have much in common, and are readily nosed in the lobby. Passion, in sum, is a leveller. Hence, the novelist's itch to express character without rise or fall in blood pressure—to bring out the individuality of the hero by subtle pictures of him changing his socks or putting in his clutch; of the heroine, by refining on her as she applies her lip-stick, pours in her bath-salts, or leans out of the window into the summer night.

This undramatic mode has its drawbacks, and, so far perhaps, only two writers, neither of whom ever wrote a novel, have succeeded in using it to perfection—the Russian Tchehov and the English Katherine Mansfield. Their stories have a real pastmastership of everyday moments, of significant insignificances, and of differentiation through little in-between events. But by both of them this in-between method of expression was instinctively, I think, rather than self-consciously, adopted. It may be doubted whether they knew quite what they were aiming at—though certain words in Katherine Mansfield's diary show that she was approaching that knowledge when she passed from the world she loved and studied.

Among the experimentalists in expression, we cannot avoid noting, also, the psycho-analyst with his, or generally her, love of the worm in the bud, and prepossession with the past; an industrious and interesting method presided over by conscience in azure stockings and a handkerchief slightly scented with iodoform. These and other experimentalists have no doubt made an arrangement with Time to pass them through the Customs. But will they all escape confiscation? I quote a couple of paragraphs chosen at random from the work of a transatlantic writer, because a rising—nay, a risen—compatriot has termed her the most important pioneer in the field of letters in his time:

"When she was quite a young one she knew she had been in a family living and that that family living was one that any one could be one not have been having if they were to be one being one not thinking about being one having been having family living."

And this:

"All there is of more chances is in a book, all there is of any more chances is in a list, all there is of chances is in an address, all there is is what is the best place not to remain sitting, and suggesting that there is no title for relieving rising."

All modern writing, we are told by her compatriot, has sprung from experiments like these. Let me, however, read you a sentence written within twelve months by a writer, not ancient, who veils himself under the initials "Y.Y.":

"Hence I shall do my best to go on thinking well of hermit crabs. They are toys—grotesques that might be fitted into a fairy's thimble—as they traffic hither and thither with their borrowed houses on their backs, while the spotted jelly-fishes float above them in their long draperies and indolence."

Dare I profess to you my preference for this, and my doubt whether, modern though it be, it has any relation to those lauded experiments?

These samples, by the way, illustrate conveniently my opening axiom that the soul of good expression is an unexpectedness which still keeps to the mark of meaning, and does not betray truth. "In their long draperies and indolence"—of jelly-fish, how unexpected, and yet how true! But what of unexpectedness lies in those other quotations comes, it would seem, from a sedulous desire to be unexpected and futuristic at all costs.

This cult of the Future in art and letters! Futuristic! The very word is self-conscious. It suggests exhaustion of interest, and folk who won't be happy till they get the moon, and when they do are still more miserable. The true discoverer is of his own day absorbed in what he is doing. He stumbles upon novelty; and his nose is not turned up. But in the effort to free English from the tiresome habit of being contemporary, experiment in expression can step backwards instead of attempting to skip. In an age of newspapers, advertisements, captions, and political speeches, revolt against everyday expression is natural. With so much froth on the lips of contemporary style, young Hopeful suffers from reaction and walks, bowing, backwards. I have in mind a recent instance—an ingenious and polished piece of work wrought in the English of an old master. A sort of pleasant false step that can be taken once with great effect, but cannot be repeated. For, however agreeable by way of a change may be the ring of older English, and however natural the surfeit in young critics of modern work, the fact remains that all great writers have made their names by expressing themselves in the diction, not of the past, but of their own day. Like the black footmen in the burlesque "Polly," we are all condemned to sing: "No retreat, no retreat; they must conquer or die who have no retreat." A little crossing with older English styles may do our modern English no harm, but the best writing of our time keeps itself supple and free from imitations, and endeavours, without mannerism, to express in words that ring new the writer's own temperament and vision. The great styles of the past cannot in the nature of things have a living unexpectedness for us of the present.

In sum, the less we try to form our English by self-conscious and definite experiments, keep our minds set towards the fresh, clear, supple expression of our visions, thoughts, and feelings, the greater the chance our English has of being fine. I make an exception, however, in favour of Income Tax forms and Acts of Parliament. A little self-conscious experiment on the part of their framers might at least enable us to understand them. Let me read you, at random, from a certain Lunacy Act:

"If, in the case of a lunatic being in a workhouse, the medical officer thereof does not sign such certificate as in sub-section 1, of this section mentioned, or if at or before the expiration of fourteen days from the date of the certificate an order is not made under the hand of a Justice for the detention of the lunatic in the workhouse, or if after such an order has been made the lunatic ceases to be a proper person to be detained in a workhouse, the medical officer of the workhouse shall forthwith give notice in writing to a relieving officer of the Union to which the workhouse belongs that a pauper in the workhouse is a lunatic and a proper person to be sent to an asylum, and thereupon the like proceedings shall be taken by the relieving officer and all other persons for the purpose of removing the lunatic to an asylum, and within the same time, as by this Act provided in the case of a pauper deemed to be a lunatic and a proper person to be sent to an asylum, and pending such proceedings the lunatic may be detained in the workhouse."

Through long and painful study I can assure you that this really has a meaning; but is it any wonder that our asylums are full?

That breathless example of expression, by the way, dates from 1890, and I suggest that we can reasonably trace to it certain stopless modern experiments. Mark the rich crescendo of tumult towards the end, and the long periods for which one must sit with head in hands before glimmer of meaning will enter into it.

In short, expression, whether of laws, psychology, episode, or feeling, should be humane, and refrain from torturing the wits of mankind.

From Acts of Parliament it seems natural to turn to Shakespeare. Has Shakespeare inspired or discouraged the writer of English? His genius exhausted, as it were, the possibilities of expression. He even gave us our slang. When we say of a bore "Fire him out!" we do but follow Shakespeare. And that takes me off at a tangent. The incorporation of slang words—local, professional, even "family" slang words—into the language is, in reason, no bad thing. Slang is, at least, vigorous and apt. Probably most of our vital words were once slang; one by one timidly made sacrosanct in despite of ecclesiastical and other wraths. For the beauty of a slang word is that you need not put it in the dictionary, it cries its own meaning to its own muffin-bell.

The mention of slang bends the mind almost insensibly towards the great American language; for some, as you know, have claimed that the Americans already have a language of their own. Let us avoid hyperbole. If Americans, with some exceptions, speak American, they still write English, and generally very good English. Compare the dialogue, for instance, in Sinclair Lewis's *Babbitt*, with the prose that lies in between; or listen to a play by Eugene O'Neill, and then peruse the polished periods of the late President Wilson. Certain Americanisms, too, are but Anglicisms which time has murdered for us. Take for example the expression "His first book *in* three years," where we should say "His first book *for* three years." "I determined not to play again *in* three months" may be met with in the early Jacobean diary of Lady Anne Clifford. Other "Americanisms" are English dialect words almost lost over here; the very common Americanism "dinky" will fall from the lips of a Dartmoor farmer, than whom no one knows less of America.

We English have quite as much divergence between our spoken and our written language, with this difference perhaps: Americans who talk in jargon often write good English; but Britons who speak the wondrous treble called cockney, and the blurred ground-bass of the Yorkshire and Lancashire towns, rarely express themselves at all in written words. And yet dare we condemn cockney—a lingo whose waters, in Southern England, seem fast flooding in over the dykes of the so-called Oxford accent, and such other rural dialects as are left?

And this brings me to a rather serious point: There is perhaps no greater divider of society than the difference in viva voce expression. If the East End on Hampstead

Heath of a Bank Holiday pronounced its aitches, and said "Bai Jove! Isn't it ráther naice?"—or if, on the other hand, the West End dropped its aitches, and said "Aow! Look at the caows in the tryne!" should we not be very near to a social millennium? And this seems to invite the further question: Which of these two forms of English, cockney twang or the drawl of culchah, is the more desirable as a national form of speech? The spirit of the age seems to favour cockney; and, certainly, it is glibber on the tongue. Place the offspring of culchad ducks under a cockney-speaking hen, and the ducklings will take to cockney as steel flies to a magnet. Cockney is infectious because it follows the line of least resistance, requiring far less effort of lips and tongue. Against cockney, then, with such adventitious advantages, the appeal must lie to the ear. To which of these two forms of speech is it pleasanter, or—shall we say—less maddening, to listen? If an unprejudiced Zulu were dropped into two circles of chatterers, the one in coster-town, the other in—well, not Oxford, for Oxford is maligned—what would be the poor fellow's verdict? Who shall say?

At the present rate of cockney progress it will, however, not be long before your presidential address opens like this:

"A meriner navigytin' the endless waters of the gry Etlentic in a Canydian canoe could feel no more lorst than the speaker venturin' on a stunt laike this. An' yet aow pleasant to know that it daon't metter aow yer steer, for in no kyse can yer arrive."

If this is not desirable, our educational authorities will have to take in hand, even more seriously than at present, the subjugation of cockney in our national schools. And yet, would it be better if your milkman's boy said every morning: "Heah you are! A quart of milk, half a pound of buttah, and a bushel of eggs? That raight? Really! I'm frightfully bucked. Goodbay!"

Perhaps some day our educational authorities may make both these forms of linguistic disease notifiable, and isolate the sufferers.

In the course of this digression I have mentioned the ear; and you will perhaps forgive me if I side-slip abruptly to the relative importance of ear and mind in lyric expression.

Take Shakespeare's "Out, out, brief candle!" Why is it charmed? Because of the vowel sounds? Or the dramatic unexpectedness of "brief" applied to "candle"? Or the image of the human spirit burning like a little flame, and blown into nothingness? Because of all three, I think, and in about equal proportions.

Or take Shelley's:

> "Mary dear, come to me soon,
> I am not well whilst thou art far;
> As sunset to the spheréd moon,
> As twilight to the western star,
> Thou, beloved, art to me."

Again the vowel sounds; the unexpectedness of the word "far"; the imagery: to these must be added the emotion of longing. Wise, by the way, is a lyric poet when his appeal is short. Even Shelley would have been accounted far greater if he had left behind him only a picked tenth of his work. Lyric expression, in fact, can never afford to outrun its own strangeness. The following sonnet of Masefield's seems to me a fine expression of strange beauty:

> "Go spend your penny, Beauty, when you will,
> In the grave's darkness let the stamp be lost.
> The water still will bubble from the hill,
> And April quick the meadows with her ghost;
> Over the grass the daffodils will shiver,
> The primroses with their pale beauty abound,
> The blackbird be a lover, and make quiver
> With his glad singing the great soul of the ground;
> So that if the body rot, it will not matter;
> Up in the earth the great game will go on,
> The coming of Spring and the running of the water,
> And the young things glad of the womb's darkness gone.
> And the joy we felt will be a part of the glory
> In the lover's kiss that makes the old couple's story."

Though the last two lines exemplify—to me at least—that sudden emotional failure which blurs so much lyrical expression, even of the best poets.

The name Masefield brings up that form of expression known as the narrative poem. How far can verse do justice to a tale? The *Iliad,* the *Odyssey,* the *Canterbury Tales* were free from the rivalry of prose, for the prose narrative did not then apparently exist. The narrative poem to-day is a hybrid—like opera, that offspring of an unhappy marriage, for drama demands swiftness, music requires luxurious leisure; and a rich, long-drawn insistence at the top of the voice on emotions essentially sudden is characteristic of their child opera. Still, some mongrels are enchanting; who can resist the seduction of *Orfeo,* of *Carmen,* of *Pagliacci?* Opera "comes off" now and again, so does the narrative poem. It is, no doubt, a question of proportion. Just as water is H2O, not H3O—unless, indeed, it has changed in these impatient times—so a narrative poem must be just rightly balanced between the lyrical and the merely narrational. If there be too little percentage of lyrical beauty, we ask ourselves why, for the telling of a tale, verse, with its metrical handicap, was chosen, when free prose was to hand. Yet none of us would have *The Ancient Mariner*—that almost perfect narrative poem—expressed in prose: it is unthinkable.

> "The moving Moon went up the sky,
> And nowhere did abide;
> Softly she was going up,
> And a star or two beside—"

Unneighbourly people—poets! Using metres so perfectly that no one can use them again! An injunction should surely have been obtained to restrain George Meredith from writing *Love in the Valley*.

> "When her mother tends her before the laughing mirror,
> Tying up her laces, looping up her curls—"

he jumped the claim of that metre in perpetuity. We owe grudges, too, against Fitzgerald for *Omar Khayyám* and Housman for *The Shropshire Lad;* and we never know when the next appropriation will be made. This is why poets have nervy temperaments, and more careful men go into the Law.

And while on the subject of lyrical expression it would seem fitting to consider what is known as journalese. Many journalists, of course, never stain their pages with that peculiar lyricism. And yet no event, I suppose, of dramatic moment occurs without the Press somewhere inflating the word-currency. The symptoms of journalese are the free use of clichés, and of artificial stimulation, through over-expression, gross or slight. It loves to say "largely," and that dreadful preposition "as regards," it dotes on any word with "cata" in it—catastrophe, cataclysm; battens on national fevers, and plays no small part in keeping a country's temperature above normal. It is highly infectious, and has been known to attack statesmen and other dignitaries. When journalese was at its rifest the Ministry of Health was established—possibly a coincidence.

But all over-expression, whether by journalists, poets, novelists, or clergymen, is bad for the language, bad for the mind; and by overexpression I mean the use of words running beyond the sincere feeling of writer or speaker or beyond what the event will sanely carry. From time to time a crusade is preached against it from the text: "The cat was on the mat." Some Victorian scribe, we must suppose, once wrote: "Stretching herself with feline grace, and emitting those sounds immemorially connected with satisfaction, Grimalkin lay on a rug whose richly variegated pattern spoke eloquently of the Orient and all the wonders of the Arabian Nights." And an exasperated reader annotated the margin with that shorter version of the absorbing event. How the late Georgian scribe will express the occurrence we do not yet know. Thus, perhaps: "What there is of cat is cat is what of cat there lying cat is what on what of mat lying cat." The reader will probably annotate the margin with "Some cat!"

But besides the verbose and florid runs another form of journalistic over-expression—the snappy head-line, which has attained as yet greater perfection in the glad atmosphere of America:

"Girl of thirteen, denied fine garb, tries death leap."

"Navy Board Holds Oil Quiz."

"Jokes on me says Angel of Film Star."

"Old man Stork a busy bird in Ruhr district."

"Acquitted murderer is through with girls."

"John T. King Highball hits Town."

Behind such galopading England still trails with leaden foot, hoping each year to overtake. "Hotspurs beat Blackburns" may yet become "Hots belt Blacks"; "Crippen hanged", "Ole man Crippen treads ether"; "Lord Palmerston unwell," "Pam punctured."

And is this perhaps the fitting moment to say a word about expression at Westminster? Eloquence, impromptu or prepared, is a gift, which fills one, who lacks it, with a sort of reverence. And yet there is no denying that rhetoric is glib of tongue and knows not suspense. While rigmarole —like a man in a fog—goes round and round in a circle. Experience, listening, and reading suggests that the hypodermic syringe alone could put a period to rigmarole in a certain house. All a man has to say on a given subject can be said—they tell us—in twenty minutes. That is why I am taking an hour!—The dictum, in other words, is an exaggeration. Still, the biographies of statesmen abound in praises of superb orations; but when you read them you are often bored to tears by their prolixity, and wonder where those biographers could have been "raised." Chatham, Burke, Fox, Grattan, Bright, Gladstone, Disraeli—there is not one who did not constantly over-express himself and weaken the pith of his persuasion. Making every allowance for the customs of a House where Bills can still, it seems, be talked out, and members are obliged to speak lest other members should speak in place of them, there is still a rich margin of need for that considered brevity which, if not the soul of wit, is at least an aid to good and vigorous English, and a guarantee against sleep.

Having said so much about over-expression, you will expect me perhaps to touch on its antithesis. We English, for all our habit of dropping into poetry, are supposed to be an inexpressive race. There is some evidence. Consider, for instance, the Englishman speaking after dinner. He hums and haas, his eyes stare vacantly, he twiddles his buttons; and then, just as you are getting nervous that he is going to break down, you become conscious of a steady stream of sound; you are relieved, you lean back; you say "Hear, hear!" and the stream flows on, neither rising nor falling, just flowing, flowing; and slowly, slowly, you become nervous again—you look at your watch—oughtn't-er-oughtn't it to stop? But it-er-doesn't. Every five minutes you rouse yourself and murmur "Ha-ha!" And the stream flows on. You give it up, you sleep, and suddenly you hear: "But, ladies and gentlemen, I must not take up any more of your time." You rap the table, you seize your glass. But—lo!—he's off again! You apostrophise the Deity in French; you yawn. He sees you, but it only seems to quicken the stream. And then, all at once, it stops. It has dried up, he is sitting down. And what has he said? What *has* he said? It has been a perfect example of under-expression.

But give an Englishman something to *do* in which he believes—for who can believe in speaking after dinner?—and he will do it with a minimum of talk; he will give you, in fact, another perfect example of verbal failure. Some few years ago painters coined the word "expressionism." When asked what they meant by it, they became involved and hot. Only fools—they thought—could mistake their meaning. Amazing number of fools in those days! At last a great good painter made it clear. Expressionism meant expressing the inside of a phenomenon without depicting its outside in a way that could be recognised. That is to say, if you wanted to express an apple-tree you drew and coloured one vertical and three fairly horizontal lines, attached a small coloured circle to one of these, and wrote the word "Fruity" in the catalogue. To express an Englishman by the expressionistic method you drew what resembled a pump, coloured it in a subdued manner, and wrote the words "Not working properly" in the catalogue.

I have not said anything, so far, about dramatic expression. The subject is delicate. When seeing a play, I am curiously absorbed in the dialogue—the interest, emotions, and suspense aroused by it. However birds may sing, streams flow, and thunders roll, on the stage; however luridly, austerely, symbolically, classically, or realistically the scene be architectured, I am seeking the human figure and the words of his mouth—the "Out, out, brief candle!" And this is unfortunate, because dramatic expression through mere words seems to be going out of fashion. Cinema, revue, ballet, puppet show, and the architectural designer—all are in conspiracy to lower its importance. When enjoying a film, a ballet, a book by Mr. Gordon Craig I become uneasy. What if words are doomed—merely to be used to fill in the interstices of architecture, the intervals between jazz music, or just written on a board! What if the dramatist is to become second fiddler, a hack hired and commissioned! Shakespeare remarked: "The play's the thing!" We echo the saying, feel virtuous, and take our tickets for "The Three-Cornered Hat," "Lilac Time," "Charlie Chaplin," and "The Follies"; or, bemoaning the absence of British drama, sit down to wait for a National Theatre.

Do not, I beg, misunderstand me! Dialogue can be intolerable. Out of whole plays by noted dramatists half the words could be blotted with advantage. Many fourth acts would be better returned to the limbo of their authors' brains. And many characters have perished of their creators' theoretical loquacity! I stand by the definition I once gave, so rashly, for it has been accusing me of failure ever since: "Good dialogue is character. . . . The art of writing true dramatic dialogue is an austere art, denying itself all licence, grudging every sentence devoted to the mere machinery of the play, suppressing all jokes and epigrams severed from character, relying for fun and pathos on the fun and tears of life. From start to finish, good dialogue is hand-made, like good lace; clear, of fine texture, furthering with each thread the harmony and strength of a design to which all must be subordinated."

It is curiously symptomatic of our variegated epoch that alongside the movement against dialogue plays are now and then written more full of polished and subtle conversation than ever plays have been. Such plays, however, though very interesting to read, hardly come under the heading of dramatic expression; they belong rather to a new form of psychological literature, intended, if not intentionally, for the study.

After all, there is no end to the extension of form—to the moulds into which we may run this language of ours, the greatest medium of expression in the world to-day. Including its American variety, the English language is the word-coin of well-nigh one hundred and seventy million white people, spread over nearly half the land surface of the earth. It is the language of practically every sea; the official tongue of some three hundred and fifty million brown and black and yellow people; the accredited business medium of the world; and more and more taught in South America, Japan, and some European countries. It would appear, indeed, to have a certain start of the artificial languages, Esperanto, Volapuk, and Ido, in the race for the honour of becoming the second language used in every country.

Now, the peace of the world and the march of true civilisation are intimately wrapped up with the exchange of international thought and the establishment of a single intercommunicating speech common to the educated in all countries. In days when hardly any orator succeeds in reseating himself without mentioning the peace of the world, I am waiting for a word in favour of that peace-promoter, the adoption in common of a second language. When educated expression in all countries finds the means of direct linguistic communication, the Cinderella, Peace, may have, at last, some chance of appearing at the ball.

The most beneficent task which the League of Nations could perform would be the conjuring of an arrangement to this end from the peoples of the earth. The ideal course is an adoption by agreement of a single second language to be taught in all countries. And I regret profoundly that there seems little likelihood of any such consummation.

The establishment of a second language, so far as present indications point, appears to rest rather upon the drift of accidental —or shall we say of natural?—causes, as an unconscious matter of practical expediency and by way of the line of least resistance. And any impartial scrutiny must at this moment of time place English at the head of all languages as the most likely to become, in a natural unforced way, the single inter-communicating tongue. There is a tide in the affairs of language as in the affairs of men. The Napoleonic wars left French the predominant medium of mental exchange. French is still perhaps the leading speech in Europe. But French will never now spread effectively by natural means beyond Europe and North Africa. The decline of Europe, the expansion of the British Empire, the magnetism and ever-increasing power of America, are making English the real world-language. Its tide was never before so high. This is a solemn thought for us who believe in our mother tongue and all it stands for—our hopes, our learning, our customs, our history, and our dreams.

For us private English folk who directly or indirectly are concerned with the welfare of the English language, there seems to be the duty of never losing sight of its world destiny. Surely we are not entitled to the slippered, unbraced word-garb of stay-at-homes; we need the attire of language braced and brushed, and fit to meet all glances. For our language is on view as never language was.

I often wonder, if only I didn't know English, what I should think of the sound of it, well talked. I believe I should esteem it a soft speech very pleasant to the ear, varied but unemphatic, singularly free from guttural or metallic sounds, restful, dignified, and friendly. I believe—how prejudiced one is!—that I would choose it, well spoken, before any language in the world, not indeed as the most beautiful, but as the medium of expression of which one would tire last. Blend though it be, hybrid between two main stocks, and tinctured by many a visiting word, it has acquired rich harmony of its own, a vigorous individuality. It is worthy of any destiny, however wide.

The mind, taking a bird's-eye view of the

English language from Chaucer to this day, noting the gradual but amazing changes it has undergone, will find it impossible, I think, to give the palm to any particular period in all those centuries. As with the lover of flowers who, through the moving seasons of the year, walks in his garden, watching the tulip and the apple blossom, the lilac, the iris, and the rose bloom in their good time, and cannot tell which most delights his eyes, nor when his garden reaches its full sweetness, so it is with us who love good English. Chaucer, Shakespeare, the makers of the Authorised Version, Defoe, Swift, Addison, Johnson, Burke, or Bright, you cannot crown the English of any one of these and say "Here the pinnacle was definitely reached." They were masters of expression, they used supremely well the English language of their days, tuning the instrument for their contemporaries, enlarging it for those who came after them. But the possibilities of this great organ of expression transcend even Shakespeare or the Bible. Dare we say that English is past its prime? Shall we accept defeat, and write the word decadent across the page? We cannot judge as yet the English of our day: we see the trees delicate or rank, leafy or dead in its bewildering wood, but the wood itself we cannot see. Every generation, and especially every English generation, is tempted to depreciate itself. This habit, however amiable and wholesome, is insincere, for there is in nearly all of us that which secretly stands by the age we live in.

I, at least, like to regard the English language as still in the making, capable of new twists and bold captures; and yet I think our attitude towards it should have more reverence; that we should love our mother tongue as we love our country, and try to express ourselves with vigour, dignity, and grace.

And so I end this wandering discourse with an affirmation of belief in the vitality, variety, the supple strength and subtle tones of our rich and ancient language; and of a hope that we may come to use it, man for man, woman for woman, speaking and writing, throughout our island, better than it has ever yet been used, with a fuller sense of its music and expressive power.

1924.

REMINISCENCES OF CONRAD

REMINISCENCES OF CONRAD

MANY writers knew my dead friend, and will write of him better than I; but no other writer knew him quite so long, or knew him both as sailor and novelist.

It was in March 1893 that I first met Conrad on board the English sailing ship "Torrens" in Adelaide Harbour. He was superintending the stowage of cargo. Very dark he looked in the burning sunlight—tanned, with a peaked brown beard, almost black hair, and dark brown eyes, over which the lids were deeply folded. He was thin, not tall, his arms very long, his shoulders broad, his head set rather forward. He spoke to me with a strong foreign accent. He seemed to me strange on an English ship. For fifty-six days I sailed in his company.

The chief mate bears the main burden of a sailing ship. All the first night he was fighting a fire in the hold. None of us seventeen passengers knew of it till long after. It was he who had most truck with the tail of that hurricane off the Leeuwin, and later with another storm. He was a good seaman, watchful of the weather, quick in handling the ship; considerate with the apprentices—we had a long, unhappy Belgian youth among them, who took unhandily to the sea and dreaded going aloft; Conrad compassionately spared him all he could. With the crew he was popular; they were individuals to him, not a mere gang; and long after he would talk of this or that among them, especially of old Andy the sailmaker: "I likéd that old fellow, you know." He was friendly with the young second mate, a cheerful, capable young seaman, very English; and respectful, if faintly ironic, with his whiskered, stout old English captain. I, supposed to be studying navigation for the Admiralty Bar, would every day work out the position of the ship with the captain. On one side of the saloon table we would sit and check our observations with those of Conrad, who from the other side of the table would look at us a little quizzically. For Conrad had commanded ships, and his subordinate position on the "Torrens" was only due to the fact that he was then still convalescent from the Congo experience which had nearly killed him. Many evening watches in fine weather we spent on the poop. Ever the great teller of a tale, he had already nearly twenty years of tales to tell. Tales of ships and storms, of Polish revolution, of his youthful Carlist gun-running adventure, of the Malay seas, and the Congo; and of men and men: all to a listener who had the insatiability of a twenty-five-year-old.

When, seven or eight years later, Conrad, though then in his best period and long acclaimed a great writer by the few, was struggling, year in year out, to keep a roof over him amidst the apathy of the many who afterwards fell over each other to read him in his worst period, I remember urging him to raise the wind by tale-telling in public. He wouldn't and he was right. Still, so incomparable a *raconteur* must have made a success, even though his audience might have missed many words owing to his strange yet fascinating accent.

On that ship he talked of life, not literature; and it is *not* true that I introduced him to the life of letters. At Cape Town, on my last evening, he asked me to his cabin, and I remember feeling that he outweighed for me all the other experiences of that voyage. Fascination was Conrad's great characteristic—the fascination of vivid expressiveness and zest, of his deeply affectionate heart, and his far-ranging subtle mind. He was extraordinarily perceptive and receptive. If we remember his portraits of the simple Englishmen of action—the inexpressive Creightons, McWhirrs, Lingards, Bakers, Allistouns, and the half-savage figures of some of his books, we get some conception of the width of his sympathies by reading the following passages in a letter to me of February 1899 on the work of Henry James:

"Technical perfection, unless there is some real glow to illumine and warm it from within, must necessarily be cold. I argue that in Henry James there is such a glow, and not a dim one either; but to us, used, absolutely accustomed, to unartistic expression of fine headlong honest (or dishonest) sentiments, the art of Henry James does appear heartless. The outlines are so clear, the figures so finished, chiselled, carved and brought out, that we exclaim—we, used to the shades of the contemporary fiction, to the more or less malformed shades—we exclaim: 'Stone!' Not at all. I say flesh and blood—very perfectly presented—perhaps with too much perfection of *method*. . . . His heart shows itself in the delicacy of his handling. . . . He is never in deep gloom or in violent sunshine. But he feels deeply and vividly every delicate shade. We cannot ask for more. Not everyone is a Turgeniew. Moreover, Turgeniew is not civilised (therein much of his charm for us) in the sense Henry James is civilised. *Satis*."

From these sensitive words it is clear that he appreciated the super-subtle, the ultra-civilised as completely as he grasped the life and thoughts of simple folk. And yet there is not, so far as I can remember, a single portrait in his gallery of a really subtle English type, for Marlowe, though English in name, is not so in nature.

Between his voyages in those last days of his sailor's life Conrad used to stay at rooms in Gillingham Street, near Victoria Station. It was there that he read so prodigiously, and there that he suffered from bouts of that lingering Congo fever which dogged his health and fastened a deep, fitful gloom over his spirit. In a letter to me he once said: "I don't say anything of actual bodily pain, for, God is my witness, I care for that less than nothing." He was, indeed, truly stoical, and his naturally buoyant spirit reacted with extreme suddenness. But all the years I knew him—thirty-one—he had to fight for decent health. Such words as "I have been abominably ill—abominably is the right word," occur again and again in his letters, and his creative achievement in a language not native to him, in face of these constant bouts of illness, approaches the marvellous.

It was the sea that gave Conrad to the English language. A fortunate accident—for he knew French better than English at that time. He started his manhood, as it were, at Marseilles. In a letter to me (1905) he says: "In Marseilles I did begin life thirty-one years ago. It's the place where the puppy opened his eyes." He was ever more at home with French literature than with English, spoke that language with less accent, liked Frenchmen, and better understood their clearer thoughts. And yet, perhaps, not quite an accident; for after all he had the roving quality which has made the English the great sea nation of the world; and, I suppose, instinct led him to seek in English ships the fullest field of expression for his nature. England, too, was to him the romantic country; it had been enshrined for him, as a boy in Poland, by Charles Dickens, Captain Marryat, Captain Cook, and Franklin the Arctic explorer. He always spoke of Dickens with the affection we have for the writers who captivate our youth.

No one, I take it, ever read the earliest Conrad without the bewildered fascination of one opening eyes on a new world; without, in fact, the feeling he himself describes in that passage of *Youth,* where he wakes up in the open boat in his first Eastern port, and sees "the East looking at him." I doubt if he will ever be surpassed as a creator of what we Westerners term "exotic atmosphere." The Malay coasts and rivers of *Almayer's Folly, An Outcast of the Islands* and the first pages of *The Rescue;* the Congo of *Heart of Darkness;* the Central Southern America of *Nostromo,* with many other land and seascapes, are bits of atmospheric painting *in excelsis.* Only one expression adequately describes the sensations of us who read *Almayer's Folly* in 1894. We rubbed our eyes. Conrad was critically accepted from the very start; he never published a book that did not rouse a chorus of praise; but it was twenty years before he was welcomed by the public with sufficient warmth to give him a decent income.

Chance, in 1914—an indifferent Conrad—at last brought him fortune. From that year on to the end his books sold well; yet, with the exception of *The Secret Sharer* and some parts of *Victory*, none of his work in that late period was up to his own exalted mark. Was it natural that popular success should have coincided with the lesser excellence? or was it simply an example of how long the strange takes to pierce the pickled hide of the reader of fiction?

It does disservice to Conrad's memory to be indiscriminate in praise of his work. Already, in reaction from this wholesale laudation, one notices a tendency in the younger generation to tilt the nose skyward and talk of his "parade." The shining work of his great period was before their time; it places him among the finest writers of all ages. Conrad's work, from *An Outcast of the Islands* to *The Secret Agent*, his work in *The Secret Sharer*, in the first chapters of *The Rescue* (written in 1898), and of some portions of *Victory*, are to his work in *The Arrow of Gold* and the last part of *The Rescue* as the value of pearl to that of mother-of-pearl. He was very tired toward the end; he wore himself clean out. To judge him by tired work is absurd; to lump all his work together, as if he were always the same Conrad, imperils a just estimate of his greatness.

I first re-encountered Conrad some months after that voyage when we paid a visit together to *Carmen* at Covent Garden Opera. *Carmen* was a vice with us both. It was already his fourteenth time of seeing that really dramatic opera. The blare of Wagner left him as cold as it leaves me; but he shared with my own father a curious fancy for Meyerbeer. In June 1910 he wrote: "I suppose I am now the only human being in these islands who thinks Meyerbeer a great composer; and I am an alien at that, and not to be wholly trusted." But music, fond though he was of it, could play no great part in a life spent at sea, and, after his marriage in 1895, in the country. He went up to Town but seldom. He wrote always with blood and tears and needed seclusion for it.

A spurt was characteristic of Conrad's endings; he finished most of his books in that way—his vivid nature instinctively staged itself with dramatic rushes. Moreover, all those long early years he worked under the whip-lash of sheer necessity.

A sailor and an artist, he had little sense of money. He was not of those who can budget exactly and keep within it; and anyway he had too little, however neatly budgeted. It is true that his dramatic instinct and his subtlety would take a sort of pleasure in plotting against the lack of money, but it was at best a lugubrious amusement for one who had to whip his brain along when he was tired, when he was ill, when he was almost desperate. Letter after letter, talk after talk, unfolded to me the travail of those years. He needed to be the Stoic he really was.

I used to stay with him a good deal from

1895-1905, first at Stanford in Essex and then at Stanford in Kent. He was indefatigably good to me while my own puppy's eyes were opening to literature, and I was still in the early stages of that struggle with his craft which a writer worth his salt never quite abandons.

His affectionate interest was always wholly generous. In his letters to me, two to three hundred, there is not a sentence which breaks, or even jars, the feeling that he cared that one should do good work. There is some valuable criticism, but never any impatience, and no stinting of appreciation or encouragement. He never went back on friendship. The word "loyalty" has been much used by those who write or speak of him. It has been well used. He was always loyal to what he had at heart—to his philosophy, to his work, and to his friends; he was loyal even to his dislikes (not few) and to his scorn. People talk of Conrad as an aristocrat; I think it rather a silly word to apply to him. His mother's family, the Bebrowskis, were Polish landowners; the Korzeniowskis, too, his father's family, came, I think, of landowning stock; but the word aristocrat is much too dry to fit Conrad; he had no touch with "ruling," no feeling for it, except, maybe, such as is necessary to sail a ship; he was first and last the rover and the artist, with such a first-hand knowledge of men and things that he was habitually impatient with labels and pigeon-holes, with cheap theorising and word debauchery. He stared life very much in the face, and distrusted those who didn't. Above all, he had the keen humour which spiflicates all class and catalogues, and all ideals and aspirations that are not grounded in the simplest springs of human nature. He laughed at the clichés of so-called civilisation. His sense of humour, indeed, was far greater than one might think from his work. He had an almost ferocious enjoyment of the absurd. Writing seemed to dry or sardonise his humour. But in conversation his sense of fun was much more vivid; it would leap up in the midst of gloom or worry, and take charge with a shout.

Conrad had six country homes after his

marriage, besides two temporary abodes. He wrote jestingly to my wife: "Houses are naturally rebellious and inimical to man." And, perhaps, having lived so much on ships, he really had a feeling of that sort. He certainly grew tired of them after a time.

I best remember Pent Farm—that little, very old, charming, if inconvenient farmhouse, with its great barn beyond the yard, under the lee of the almost overhanging Pent. It was a friendly dwelling where you had to mind your head in connection with beams; and from whose windows you watched ducks and cats and lambs in the meadows beyond. He liked those quiet fields and that sheltering hill. Though he was not what we should call a "lover of nature" in the sense of one who spends long hours lost in the life of birds and flowers, of animals and trees, he could be vividly impressed by the charm and the variety of such things. He was fond, too, of Hudson's books; and no lover of Hudson's work is insensible to nature.

In Conrad's study at the Pent we burned together many midnight candles, much tobacco. In that house was written some of the *Youth* volume, *Lord Jim,* most of the *Typhoon* volume, *Nostromo, The Mirror of the Sea, The Secret Agent,* and other of Conrad's best work. Save that *The Nigger of the Narcissus* and the story *Youth* were written just before, at Stanford in Essex, the "Pent" may be said to synchronise with Conrad's best period. Kent was undoubtedly the county of his adoption, and this was the first of his four Kentish homes.

Many might suppose that Conrad would naturally settle by the sea. He never did. He had seen too much of it; like the sailor who when he turns into his bunk takes care that no sea air shall come in, he lived always well inland. The sea was no favourite with one too familiar with its moods. He disliked being labelled a novelist of the sea. He wrote of the sea, as perhaps no one, not even Herman Melville, has written; but dominant in all his writing of the sea is the note of struggle and escape. His hero is not the sea, but man in conflict with that cruel and treacherous element. Ships he loved, but the sea—no. Not that he ever abused it, or talked of it with aversion; he accepted it as he accepted all the inscrutable remorselessness of Nature. It was man's job to confront Nature with a loyal and steady heart—that was Conrad's creed, his contribution to the dignity of life. Is there a better? First and last he was interested in men, fascinated by the terrific spectacle of their struggles in a cosmos about which he had no illusions. He was sardonic, but he had none of the cynicism characteristic of small, cold-hearted beings.

He customarily laboured in the morning, and often would sit long hours over a single page. In 1906, when he was staying in our London house, he wrote to my wife: "I don't know that I am writing much in the little wooden house" (out in the garden), "but I smoke there religiously for three and a half hours every morning, with a sheet of paper before me and an American fountain-pen in my hand. What more could be expected from a conscientious author, I can't imagine."

In later years, when his enemy, gout, often attacked his writing hand, he was obliged to resort a good deal to dictation of first drafts. I cannot but believe that his work suffered from that necessity. But there were other and increasing handicaps —the war, which he felt keenly, and those constant bouts of ill-health which dragged at his marvellous natural vitality. I think I never saw Conrad quite in repose. His hands, his feet, his knees, his lips—sensitive, expressive, and ironical—something was always in motion, the dynamo never quite at rest within him. His mind was extraordinarily active and his memory for impressions and people most retentive, so that he stored with wonderful accuracy all the observations of his dark-brown eyes, that were so piercing and yet could be so soft. He had the precious faculty of interest in detail. To that we owe his pictures of scenes and life long past—their compelling verisimilitude, the intensely vivid variety of their composition. The storehouse of his subconscious self was probably as interesting and comprehensive a museum as any in the world. It is from the material in our subconscious minds that we create. Conrad's eyes never ceased snapshotting, and the millions of photographs they took were laid away by him to draw on. Besides, he was not hampered in his natural watchfulness by the preoccupation of an egoistic personality. He was not an egoist; he had far too much curiosity and genuine interest in things and people to be that. I don't mean to say that he had not an interest in himself and a belief in his own powers. His allusions to his work are generally disparaging; but at heart he knew the value of his gifts; and he liked appreciation, especially from those (not many) in whose judgment he had faith. He received more praise, probably, than any other writer of our time; but he never suffered from that *parvenu* disease, swelled head; and "I," "I," "I" played no part in his talk.

People have speculated on the literary

influences that for him were formative. Flaubert and Henry James have been cited as his spiritual fathers. It won't do. Conrad was a most voracious reader, and he was trilingual. A Slav temperament, a life of duty and adventure, vast varied reading, and the English language—those were the elements from which his highly individual work emerged. Not I, who have so often heard him speak of them, will deny his admiration for Flaubert, de Maupassant, Turgenev, and Henry James; but one has only to read Conrad's first book, *Almayer's Folly*, to perceive that he started out on a path of his own, with a method quite peculiar to himself, involuted to a dangerous degree, perhaps, and I can trace no definite influence on him by any writer. He was as different from Henry James as East from West. Both had a certain natural intricacy and a super-psychological bent, but there the likeness stops. As for Flaubert—whom he read with constancy—that conscientious Frenchman and determined stylist could do nothing for Conrad except give him pleasure. No one could help Conrad. He had to subdue to the purposes of his imagination a language that was not native to him; to work in a medium that was not the natural clothing of his Polish temperament. There were no guides to the desert that he crossed. I think perhaps he most delighted in the writings of Turgenev; but there is not the slightest evidence that he was influenced by him. He loved Turgenev's personality, and disliked Tolstoi's. The name Dostoievsky was in the nature of a red rag to him. I am told that he once admitted that Dostoievsky was "deep as the sea." Perhaps that was why he could not bear him, or possibly it was that Dostoievsky was too imbued with Russian essence for Polish appetite. In any case, his riderless extremisms offended something deep in Conrad.

I have spoken of his affection for Dickens. Trollope he liked. Thackeray I think not over much, though he had a due regard for such creations as Major Pendennis. Meredith's characters to him were "seven feet high," and his style too inflated. He admired Hardy's poetry. He always spoke with appreciation of Howells, especially of the admirable *Rise of Silas Lapham.* His affectionate admiration for Stephen Crane we know from his introduction to Thomas Beer's biography of that gifted writer. Henry James in his middle period —the Henry James of *Daisy Miller, The Madonna of the Future, Greville Fane, The Real Thing, The Pension Beaurepas* —was precious to him. But of his feeling for that delicate master, for Anatole France, de Maupassant, Daudet, and Turgenev, he has written in his *Notes on Life and Letters.* I remember, too, that he had a great liking for those two very different writers, Balzac and Merimée.

Of philosophy he had read a good deal, but on the whole spoke little. Schopenhauer used to give him satisfaction twenty years and more ago, and he liked both the personality and the writings of William James.

I saw little of Conrad during the war. Of

whom did one see much? He was caught in Poland at the opening of that business, and it was some months before he succeeded in getting home. Tall words, such as "War to end War" left him, a continental and a realist, appropriately cold. When it was over he wrote: "So I send these few lines to convey to you both all possible good wishes for unbroken felicity in your new home and many years of peace. At the same time I'll confess that neither felicity nor peace inspire me with much confidence. There is an air of 'the packed valise' about these two divine but unfashionable figures. I suppose the North Pole would be the only place for them, where there is neither thought nor heat, where the very water is stable, and the democratic bawlings of the virtuous leaders of mankind die out into a frozen, unsympathetic silence." Conrad had always a great regard for men of action, for workmen who stuck to their last and did their own jobs well; he had a corresponding distrust of amateur omniscience and handy wiseacres; he curled his lip at political and journalistic protestation; cheap-jackery and clap-trap of all sorts drew from him a somewhat violently expressed detestation. I suppose what he most despised in life was ill-educated theory, and what he most hated, blatancy and pretence. He smelled it coming round the corner and at once his bristles would rise. He was an extremely quick judge of a man. I remember a dinner convoked by me, that he might meet a feminine compatriot of his own married to one who was not a compatriot. The instant dislike he took to that individual was so full of electricity that we did not dine in comfort. The dislike was entirely merited. This quick instinct for character and types inimical to him was balanced by equally sure predilections, so that his friendships were always, or nearly always, lasting—I can think of only one exception. He illustrated vividly the profound truth that friendship is very much an affair of nerves, grounded in instinct rather than in reason or in circumstance, the outcome of a sort of deep affinity which prevents jarring. His Preface to the *Life of Stephen Crane* supplies all the evidence we need of Conrad's instantaneous yet lasting sympathy with certain people; and of his instant antipathy to others. It contains also the assurance that after he became a writer he "never kept a diary and never owned a note-book"—a statement which surprised no one who knew the resources of his memory and the brooding nature of his creative spirit.

"Genius" has somewhere been defined as the power to make much out of little. In *Nostromo* Conrad made a continent out of just a sailor's glimpse of a South American port, some twenty years before. In *The Secret Agent* he created an underworld out of probably as little actual experience. On the other hand, we have in *The Nigger,* in *Youth* and *Heart of Darkness* the raw material of his own life transmuted into the gold of fine art. People, and there are such, who think that writers like Conrad, if there be any, can shake things from their sleeve, would be staggered if they could have watched the pain and stress of his writing life. In his last letter to me but one, February 1924, he says: "However, I have begun to work a little—on my runaway novel. I call it 'runaway' because I've been after it for two years (The Rover is a mere interlude) without being able to overtake it. The end seems as far as ever! It's like a chase in a nightmare—weird and exhausting. Your news that you have finished a novel brings me a bit of comfort. So there are novels that *can* be finished—then why not mine? Of course I see 'fiction' advertised in the papers—heaps of it. But published announcements seem to me mere phantasms. . . . I don't believe in their reality." There are dozens of such allusions to almost despairing effort in his letters. He must, like all good workmen, have had his hours of compensation; but if ever a man worked in the sweat of spirit and body it was Conrad. That is what makes his great achievement so inspiring. He hung on to his job through every kind of weather, mostly foul. He never shirked.

In an age more and more mechanical, more and more given to short cuts and the line of least resistance, the example of his life's work shines out; its instinctive fidelity, his artist's desire to make the best thing he could. Fidelity! Yes, that is the word which best sums up his life and work.

The last time I saw Conrad—about a year ago—I wasn't very well, and he came and sat in my bedroom, full of affectionate solicitude. It seems, still, hardly believable that I shall not see him again. His wife tells me that a sort of homing instinct was on him in the last month of his life, that he seemed sometimes to wish to drop everything and go back to Poland. Birth calling to Death—no more than that, perhaps, for he loved England, the home of his wandering, of his work, of his last long landfall.

If to a man's deserts is measured out the quality of his rest, Conrad shall sleep well.

1924.

TIME, TIDES, AND TASTE

TIME, TIDES, AND TASTE

THE tides of taste flow and ebb and flow again, and works of "genius" and "art" pop in and out of fashion like little men on old-time clocks. So that a watcher, even in one brief generation, acquires a wholesome cynicism, eyes dog-wise the criticism of the day, the cults of the clever, the enthusiasms of the young. He learns that experiment and achievement are not quite interchangeable terms. The shortness of life and the length of art are to him increasingly apparent, and he has come to mistrust the inveterate cockeyed cocksureness of the literary man.

Save as museum pieces in the unvisited rooms of the Past, how very few books live! In the whole range of English literature down to 1800, who, except by professors and their pupils as part of education, is widely read? Shakespeare. Save for some dozen or so still well-thumbed volumes, the others—even Chaucer, Bunyan, Milton, Dryden, Johnson, Defoe, Swift, Fielding, Jeremy Taylor—are but venerable names. Of all the great English writers, poets and novelists of the nineteenth century, who are now really *coram populo?* Dickens, Stevenson, and Mark Twain; with Shelley, Scott, Wordsworth, Jane Austen, Trollope, and Tennyson, dipped into; and the readers of such as Byron, Hawthorne, Thackeray, Poe, the Brontës, Marryat, Charles Reade, Browning, Blackmore, Artemus Ward, Whitman, Herman Melville, confined to two or three surviving books apiece. I speak not here of connoisseurs, students, or bookworms, but of the reading public at large. Even Meredith, Swinburne, Howells, and Henry James are passing already from the minds of those who read for pastime. Who among the living will fare better? Shall we not drift into dusty limbo, at best remembered as names, or each by a book or two—a *Tess,* an *Esther Waters,* a *Mr. Polly,* a *Babbitt,* an *Ethan Frome,* an *Old Wives' Tale,* a *Reynard the Fox.* And in the twilight of this reflection the number of "great" books that appear every year, the annual geniuses, have but a sober hue. The wheel turns and they fly off like the powdery dust of high summer.

In this general certainty of extinction the future is hardly worth considering by writers. We are of our day. Lamb-like, we kick our heels in the spring; and, if lucky, are still served with mint sauce, instead of currant jelly, in the autumn. On the stage, lately, they performed a skit of the high-kicking dances that adorned English Gaiety burlesques in the late eighties—a row of young women, over-rouged, over-wigged, and under-frilled, trying with an intent and solemn diligence to reach high heaven with their toes. With what utter and expressionless precision their legs went up—and up—and up! We remembered the original and the pleasure it then gave us! Dear me! Our taste had changed.

Yes, the Eighties are paved over, and the grass grows between; but they were vital while they lasted—as vital as these Twenties, who must themselves become a grass-grown walk. Remember the Nineties and their Yellow Book—how it glittered and it shone—not Solomon in all his glory put on so many frills. And where are they now? To think that these high-spirited Twenties, with their absolute taste, will be the "gone-offs" of the Thirties, the "old geysers" of the Forties! Professor Einstein, who with such careful ceremony, married relativity to a world which had in secret always enjoyed it, left to youthful æsthetes his cast-off "absolute," so that—if not precisely in unity—they might dwell together, decade by decade, unrelated in their taste to time and tide.

The first years of this century turned the moon over, too; were as absolute as these Twenties, and as clever. They met, shook a leg, put out a tongue, and lo! their elders did not exist—at least for the moment. There was Hardy! Let us see what happened to the pooı man. They labelled him old-fashioned, and out he went, but—he came in again. There was Stevenson, that mere Romantic—how many deaths he died on their lips! There was Kipling—oh, poor Kipling! There was Barrie—a sad case! There was Shaw—that shocking journalist! And then those smart young "absolutes" lost their innocence, passed into relativity, and now are the merest "geysers" themselves. There were sucking geniuses in those days, too, but they all died young, killed by the innocents who followed. Layer on layer the ages lie, each as innocent as the one before, and each happy while it lasts, under its midnight lamps, putting the Past in its place, and that a little lower than its own, monopolising style, and with serene finality pronouncing: "This is 'done,'" or "that is drivel."

Those periodic makers of new forms—canonised and pedestalled by coterie—how little they shake the world of letters! They are like novelists who enter the British House of Commons to reform society, and leave it—oh! so soon—with nothing but themselves reformed. You remember that Mr. Carlyle who purposed to renovate style? Oh! what a to-do! But when he was through, there were only his works and your smile. Since then there have been others—this decade boasts at least three—and when it passes, so will they, clad lightly in a general grin. For if anything is certain in the mystery which surrounds literary survival, it is this: The "precious" has precious little chance. Was there anything exotic, self-conscious in their day, about the expression of any among those who have eluded Time so far? Of Homer, say—if ever Homer was—or the Greek dramatists; of Virgil, Horace, Plutarch, Dante, Montaigne, Shakespeare, Cervantes, Goethe, Tolstoi? These outran no constables. That is worth a thought before falling on our knees in front of the Messieurs Petitmaitre or Madame Soubresaut. Calm, unruffled, all-absorbing, the main stream of literature flows, and makes of each little tributary decade, which takes itself for eternity, about as much as a trout makes of a single mayfly.

But the cry of literary Youth: "Crown

taste in our time, O Lord! We are 'the goods'!" is welcome. Without the two-year-olds, their breeding, paces, colour, trials, performance, the literary papers would be starved. Lacking discovery of new flyers and discovery that old flyers never could fly, contemporary criticism could not sing with Macheath:

> "I sip every flower,
> I change every hour!"

And how amusing it is to watch the wheel of criticism turning—to see a Dostoievsky displace a Turgenev, a Tchehov displace both; a Dreiser replace a Norris, a Lewis a Dreiser, Un Tel a Lewis, a Dreiser Un Tel; a Proust displace a France, and a Joyce replace the Deity!

Once on a time an English editor in a single discharge blew from his mouth every literary name alive, and died editorially in the blast. This was perhaps the most striking example of time-and-trouble-saving in all the history of literature. Why spend ten years in sapping what can be blasted in a day without any sapping at all, especially when the result is the same in both cases! For literary fame—not the brand in publishers' advertisements, nor the bay-leaf grown in cafés, but that which clings on, though blasted every other decade—is mysteriously entwined with public favour, and curiously detached from critical pronouncement. Like ivy, it gets slow hold, climbs up a writer, spreads in a mass of decorative leaf, and sometimes chokes the creative life out of him. Take the strange case of Conrad, who during the first eighteen years of his writing life was praised by critics as writers seldom have been, yet was hardly known to the public; and then, in a quick three years, was covered with the leaves of fame. Take the case of Kipling, critically acclaimed, critically condemned, again acclaimed, again condemned, and strangely famous all the time. Contemporary taste sways with action and reaction, obeys a dislike of repetition, a craving for novelty; follows the talk of the most self-conscious literary clique of its day, and swims with the tide of worldly circumstance, such as a pre-war or an after-war mood; it is policed only by a sense of proportion in the general mind, which all the time manages to rescue from the ebb and flow of taste, what really feeds and amuses it. The mental appetite of literary youth changes almost every year; the mental appetite of simpler folk remains much the same for a generation at least; and certain primal food-demands of the mind last down the centuries: Item, the craving for drama, which is satisfied by the telling of a tale; item, the craving for seeing yourself and your neighbour reproduced, which is satisfied by the creation of character. The period whose taste gets away from these simple demands is found in the long run no tributary, however it may have raced and bubbled in its own eyes, but just a backwater.

The present period, very sparkling, unquestionably self-conscious and inclined to proclaim its monopoly of cleverness, will contribute, but not by virtue of its opinion of itself, nor by reason of its extravagant experiments. The Forties will not write—nay, nor even the Thirties—in the style of Mr. Dotter and Mrs. Dasher of the Twenties; the Thirties will put in stops again, with other old-fashioned aids to the brain, such as coherence and a certain connection between words and thought. Violent changes, which are "the thing" from time to time, should at least be based on practical advantage. Take the change in dancing, for example; it has two very practical—dare we say?—advantages; it causes less perspiration, and establishes closer contact between male and female. But the stopless and the "bide-a-wee-thorn" writers of today cause more perspiration and establish a wider space between themselves and their readers. They require more time and patience but readers have ever less of both. Stopless and Bide-a-wee-thorn will end by taking in each other's washing, and with no circle of adorers to see how they do it. This, indeed, is a sure thing. But Stopless and Bide-a-wee-thorn, however earnest their own convictions that they are pioneers to a more precious future, are mere stunt customers. By them To-day will not be judged. No! To-day will count because, like most periods, it has some genuine creative talent, some real power of telling a tale, and some quiet devotion to its job. It will count in spite of that proclaimed cleverness which is perhaps only speed. The ball flies more lightly—the "wickets are faster," as we say; hit or get out is the watchword. But the result? Will Time give the palm to the team of today over the team of ten, twenty, thirty years ago? Maybe—for there never were so many players of the writing game as now. They jostle up like young larch trees planted too close together; and some will shoot ahead and be spared for a time, as ornamental timber, when the Great Forester converts the covert into pit-props.

But as to the claim, seemingly implicit in café-table talk, that some fresh human faculty has been awakened, that there is a real new demand of the mind, which the old writers, painters, and composers cannot satisfy—let us consider! Applause now greets a piece of decorative noise such as Honegger's rendering of a locomotive's progress. But even in the time of Bach would not Honegger or Stravinsky—provided they escaped incarceration—have stimulated the eighteenth-century man by their ingenious noises fully as much as the beating of forest drums has always stimulated people? Down to quite a short time ago a white man who craved for exciting noise had to repair to the Zoos at feeding-time, or hire a man to play the bagpipes without actually breaking into a tune. Such considerable and not undignified sounds were all he could obtain, but his appetite was there; all unknowingly he hungered for *Le Sacre du Printemps.* So in literature—the reader down to 1910 was forced to glut his cravings for the symptomatic and the well-nigh unintelligible, on medical treatises, and the differential calculus; now he can take down a novel.

Many who went about looking at pictures and sculpture in the last century loved also to see cranes at work, engines giving off steam, scaffolding at night-time, piles of beetroot, and the simple village pump; there was a craving within them that pictures and sculpture did not satisfy—whereas now it is different.

No, this new faculty and demand is probably *not* at all new. To-day is simply satisfying an old craving in a different and more compendious fashion. People have been known to affirm that the new music, art, literature are mere noise, pattern, and mental exercise; but that is very rude and old-fashioned! The new art, music, and literature—I speak of their exotic blossoms—satisfy certain emotional or mental desires which hitherto could get no food from art. To be able to call art that which we used not to call art must surely give us a broader satisfaction, or at least put a higher premium on our lower cravings. It widens, if it does not heighten, our conception of æstheticism, to include among the æsthetic, the child, the savage, the mathematician, the medical man—very considerable sections of the population—hitherto excluded. Probably we shall never again let these new æsthetes slip altogether from the company of the elect—though in the Thirties and Forties we may not place them quite so high in the scale of taste.

Yes, on the whole we must reject the theory of a new faculty in the modern mind, and fall back on a simple shift of categories. The human being doesn't change so quickly as all that, but labels are always getting swapped around; and, in that activity, To-day is highly active and adventurous, if possibly a little intoxicated and calisthenic. But, to risk a repetition: To-day will be remembered for more substantial reasons than its cocktails and its calisthenics. And since, in any case, like other periods, it must pass, shall it not kick as high as it can, while yet living? The certainty of decease is an incentive to vitality in the well-constituted mind. To be alive and, as Mr. Verdant Green used to say, "prou' title" is the keystone of philosophy. Let Time do his worst! The Twenties do well to defy him. For no matter how many candles they burn, judgments pronounce, or policies of insurance take out, the Old Blighter will have his way with them in the end.

1925.

FOREWORD TO "GREEN MANSIONS"

FOREWORD TO "GREEN MANSIONS"

I TAKE up pen for this foreword with the fear of one who knows that he cannot do justice to his subject, and the trembling of one who would not, for a good deal, set down words unpleasing to the eye of him who wrote *Green Mansions, The Purple Land,* and all those other books which have meant so much to me. For of all living authors—now that Tolstoi has gone—I could least dispense with W. H. Hudson. Why do I love his writing so? I think because he is, of living writers that I read, the rarest spirit, and has the clearest gift of conveying to me the nature of that spirit. Writers are to their readers little new worlds to be explored; and each traveller in the realms of literature must needs have a favourite hunting ground, which, in his good-will—or perhaps merely in his egoism—he would wish others to share with him.

The great and abiding misfortunes of most of us writers are twofold: We are, as worlds, rather common tramping ground for our readers, rather tame territory; and as guides and dragomans thereto we are too superficial, lacking clear intimacy of expression; in fact,—like guide or dragoman—we cannot let folk into the real secrets, or show them the spirit, of the land.

Now Hudson, whether in a pure romance like this *Green Mansions,* or in that romantic piece of realism *The Purple Land,* or in books like *Idle Days in Patagonia, Afoot in England, The Land's End, Adventures Among Birds, A Shepherd's Life,* and all his other nomadic records of communings with men, birds, beasts, and Nature, has a supreme gift of disclosing not only the thing he sees but the spirit of his vision. Without apparent effort he takes you with him into a rare, free, natural world, and always you are refreshed, stimulated, enlarged by going there.

He is, of course, a distinguished naturalist, probably the most acute, broad-minded and understanding observer of nature living. And this, in an age of specialism, which loves to put men into pigeon-holes and label them, has been a misfortune to the reading public, who seeing the label Naturalist, pass on and take down the nearest novel. Hudson has indeed the gifts and knowledge of a naturalist, but that is a mere fraction of his value and interest. A really great writer such as this is no more to be circumscribed by a single word than America by the part of it called New York. The expert knowledge which Hudson has of Nature gives to all his work backbone and surety of fibre, and to his sense of beauty an intimate actuality. But his real eminence and extraordinary attraction lie in his spirit and philosophy. We feel from his writings that he is nearer to Nature than other men, and yet more truly civilised. The competitive, towny culture, the queer up-to-date commercial knowingness with which we are so busy coating ourselves, simply will not stick to him. A passage in his *Hampshire Days* describes him better than I can: "The blue sky, the brown soil beneath, the grass, the trees, the animals, the wind, and rain, and stars are never strange to me; for I am in and of and am one with them; and my flesh and the soil are one, and the heat in my blood and in the sunshine are one, and the winds and the tempests and my passions are one. I feel the 'strangeness' only with regard to my fellow men, especially in towns, where they exist in conditions unnatural to me, but congenial to them. . . . In such moments we sometimes feel a kinship with, and are strangely drawn to, the dead, who were not as these; the long, long dead, the men who knew not life in towns, and felt no strangeness in sun and wind and rain." This unspoiled unity with Nature pervades all his writings; they are remote from the fret and dust and pettiness of town life; they are large, direct, free. It is not quite simplicity, for the mind of this writer is subtle and fastidious, sensitive to each motion of natural and human life; but his sensitiveness is somehow different from, almost inimical to, that of us others, who sit indoors and dip our pens in shades of feeling. Hudson's fancy is akin to the flight of the birds that are his special loves—it never seems to have entered a house, but since birth to have been roaming the air, in rain and sun, or visiting the trees and the grass. I not only disbelieve utterly, but intensely dislike, the doctrine of metempsychosis, which, if I understand it aright, seems the negation of the creative impulse, an apotheosis of staleness—nothing quite new in the world, never anything quite new—not even the soul of a baby; and so I am not prepared to entertain the whim that a bird was one of his remote incarnations; still, in sweep of wing, quickness of eye, and natural sweet strength of song he is not unlike a super-bird—which is a horrid image.

And that reminds me: This, after all, is a foreword to *Green Mansions*—the romance of the bird-girl Rima—a story actual yet fantastic, which immortalises, I think, as passionate a love of all beautiful things as ever was in the heart of man.

Somewhere Hudson says: "The sense of the beautiful is God's best gift to the human soul." So it is; and to pass that gift on to others, in such measure, as herein is expressed, must surely have been happiness to him who wrote *Green Mansions.* In form and spirit the book is unique, a simple romantic narrative transmuted by sheer glow of beauty into a prose poem. Without ever departing from its quality of a tale, it symbolises the yearning of the human soul for the attainment of perfect love and beauty in this life—that impossible perfection which we must all learn to see fall from its high tree and be consumed in the flames, as was Rima the bird-girl, but whose fine white ashes we gather that they may be mingled at last with our own, when we too have been refined by the fire of death's resignation. The book is soaked through and through with a strange beauty. I will not go on singing its praises, or trying to make it understood, because I have other words to say of its author.

Do we realise how far our town life and

culture have got away from things that really matter; how instead of making civilisation our handmaid to freedom we have set her heel on our necks, and under it bite dust all the time? Hudson, whether he knows it or not, is now the chief standard-bearer of another faith. Thus he spake in *The Purple Land*: "Ah, yes, we are all vainly seeking after happiness in the wrong way. It was with us once and ours, but we despised it, for it was only the old common happiness which Nature gives to all her children, and we went way from it in search of another grander kind of happiness which some dreamer—Bacon or another—assured us we should find. We had only to conquer Nature, find out her secrets, make her our obedient slave, then the earth would be Eden, and every man Adam and every woman Eve. We are still marching bravely on, conquering Nature, but how weary and sad we are getting! The old joy in life and gaiety of heart have vanished, though we do sometimes pause for a few moments in our long forced march to watch the labours of some pale mechanician, seeking after perpetual motion, and indulge in a little, dry, cackling laugh at his expense." And again: "For here the religion that languishes in crowded cities, or steals shamefaced to hide itself in dim churches, flourishes greatly, filling the soul with a solemn joy. Face to face with Nature on the vast hills at eventide, who does not feel himself near to the Unseen?

> "Out of his heart God shall not pass,
> His image stampèd is on every grass."

All Hudson's books breathe this spirit of revolt against our new enslavement by towns and machinery, and are true oases in an age so dreadfully resigned to the "pale mechanician."

But Hudson is not, as Tolstoi was, a conscious prophet; his spirit is freer, more wilful, whimsical—almost perverse—and far more steeped in love of beauty. If you called him a prophet he would stamp his foot at you—as he will at me if he reads these words; but his voice is prophetic, for all that, crying in a wilderness, out of which, at the call, will spring up roses here and there, and the sweet-smelling grass. I would that every man, woman, and child in England were made to read him; and I would that America would take him to heart. He is a tonic, a deep refreshing drink, with a strange and wonderful flavour; he is a mine of new interests, and ways of thought instinctively right. As a simple narrator he is well-nigh unsurpassed; as a stylist he has few, if any, living equals. And in all his work there is an indefinable freedom from any thought of after-benefit—even from the desire that we should read him. He puts down what he sees and feels, out of sheer love of the thing seen, and the emotion felt; the smell of the lamp has not touched a single page that he ever wrote. That alone is a marvel to us who know that to write well, even to write clearly, is a woundy business, long to learn, hard to learn, and no gift of the angels. Style should not obtrude between a writer and his reader; it should be servant, not master. To use words so true and simple that they oppose no obstacle to the flow of thought and feeling from mind to mind, and yet by juxtaposition of word-sounds set up in the recipient continuing emotion or gratification—this is the essence of style; and Hudson's writing has pre-eminently this double quality. From almost any page of his books an example might be taken. Here is one no better than a thousand others, a description of two little girls on a beach: "They were dressed in black frocks and scarlet blouses, which set off their beautiful small dark faces; their eyes sparkled like black diamonds, and their loose hair was a wonder to see, a black mist or cloud about their heads and necks composed of threads fine as gossamer, blacker than jet and shining like spun glass—hair that looked as if no comb or brush could ever tame its beautiful wildness. And in spirit they were what they seemed: such a wild, joyous, frolicsome spirit, with such grace and fleetness, one does not look for in human beings, but only in birds or in some small bird-like volatile mammal—a squirrel or a spider-monkey of the tropical forest, or the chinchilla of the desolate mountain slopes—the swiftest, wildest, loveliest, most airy and most vocal of small beasties." Or this, as the quintessence of a sly remark: "After that Manual got on to his horse and rode away. It was black and rainy, but he had never needed moon or lantern to find what he sought by night, whether his own house, or a fat cow—also his own, perhaps." So one might go on quoting felicity for ever from this writer. He seems to touch every string with fresh and un-inked fingers; and the secret of his power lies, I suspect, in the fact that his words "Life being more than all else to me . . ." are so utterly true.

I do not descant on his love for simple folk and simple things, his championship of the weak, and the revolt against the cagings and cruelties of life, whether to men or birds or beasts, that springs out of him as if against his will; because, having spoken of him as one with a vital philosophy or faith, I would not draw red herrings across the main trail of his worth to the world. His work is a vision of natural beauty and of human life as it might be, quickened and sweetened by the sun and the wind and the rain, and by fellowship with all the other forms of life—the truest vision now being given to us, who are more in want of it than any generation has ever been. A very great writer, and—to my thinking—the most valuable our age possesses.

1915.

A NOTE ON SENTIMENT

A NOTE ON SENTIMENT

SENTIMENT (so far as literature is concerned) may be defined, I suppose, as the just verbal expression of genuine feeling; it becomes sentimentalism when the feeling is not genuine, or when the expression strikes the reader as laid on with too thick a pen. I find a good instance of the difference in a certain novel of my own, written at a time of stress, and re-read for the first time in calm days six years later. I found it sentimental, and started to revise it. By cutting out thirty thousand words, or just one quarter of the book, without omitting or altering any of the incidents, or eliminating any of the characters, simply by chopping words out of almost every sentence and thereby removing the over-expression, I reduced the sentimentalism to sentiment, so far as I could judge.

In any definition of sentiment or sentimentalism, reader, in fact, as well as writer, is involved. That there is nothing absolute in the matter will be admitted even by holders of literary opinions canonised in coterie—nothing more absolute than in canonised opinion itself. Time plays skittles with the definitions of sentiment as freely as with the views of the criticaster. Not a Victorian novelist, English or American, save perhaps Marryat and Mark Twain, would escape being pilloried as sentimental by the sniffers of to-day. The cynic of 1870 is the sentimentalist of 1920. The sentimentalist of 1920 may become the cynic of 1970. Comparing Defoe, Fielding and Smollett with the Victorians, we see that the definition of sentiment follows the normal laws of reaction, or, perhaps more exactly, yields to the changes of education and environment. Young men or women of to-day, for example, with all their deep feelings, passions and sufferings still to come, and accustomed to the jibing prevalent where art is discussed but seldom achieved, will find almost any verbal expression of feeling "sentimental," while a farmer's wife, who would never in voice or vocabulary do ten per cent. of justice to any emotion she might feel, will be approvingly stirred by a treacly situation in play or film, and shed tears over extravagantly false pathos in the books she reads. Nor can it be assumed that the more highly educated a person, the thinner the pen he demands of the writer who is expressing feeling. A Gilbert Murray may sometimes be moved by what a sucking poet would call "sentimental tosh!" In fact, there are all sorts of complications. There are readers, for instance, who hold that literature should not stir emotion in any way connected with life, but only rouse a kind of gloating sensation in the brain, and such readers—the equivalent of the old "æsthetes"—are highly vocal. There is the type of critic, with whom certain sorts of emotional expression, however thickly traced, escape the charge "sentimental" because connected with "the sportsman and the gentleman," but to whom certain other kinds are "slop," because not so well connected. There is the complication of the label. Label an author sentimental, and whatever he writes is sentimental, whether it really is or not. And, finally, every writer who expresses feeling at all has his own particular unconscious point of over-expression. Thomas Hardy, Joseph Conrad, even Bernard Shaw—not as a rule laid under this charge—can be sentimental in their own particular ways. The whole subject is intricate; nor is it helpful that what is sentimental to an Englishman is not sentimental to a Frenchman, and so forth.

Still, it may be laid down with some certainty that a writer must give adequate expression to his genuine feeling, or he will not be worth reading. And the whole matter lies in that word adequate. Let me cite four random examples of what I, at least, consider adequate verbal expression of true feeling: The poem called "The Bull," by Ralph Hodgson; the few pages describing the death of Bazarov in Turgenev's *Fathers and Children;* a story called "Life of Ma Parker," in Katherine Mansfield's volume

Bliss; Thomas Hardy's little poem called "Afterwards," from the collection *Moments of Vision.* Adopting this test of *adequacy* the word sentimental, then, should only be applied where expression runs ahead of the writer's real feeling—in other words, in cases of insincerity, conscious or unconscious. The unconscious cases are, of course, the most common. Who does not know the auto-intoxications and hypnotisations by feeling, indulgence in which one's steadier sense afterwards repugns? But there is danger in too great readiness to pour cold water on the intoxications, whether of self or others. Juice and generosity in verbal expression are possibly more healthy than the under-expression of those afraid to give themselves away. There is a certain meanness in a dry and trained attitude of superiority to emotion, and in that slug-like temperament which prides itself on cold-bloodedness. English training is especially self-conscious. At root, perhaps a matter of climate; but in later stages, due to our public schools and universities, which strangely influence at second-hand classes not in direct touch with them. The guiding principle of English life and education is a stoicism discouraging all exhibition of emotion, and involving a high degree of self-control. For practical ends it has great value; for the expression and appreciation of art or literature, extremely little. It warps the critical point of view, removing it from an emotional to an ethical and practical basis. To indulge in emotional expression is bad for manners, for progress, trade, and will-power; and, freely using the word sentimental, we stamp on the habit. But art of any kind is based on emotion, and can only be duly apprehended through the emotional faculties. Letting these atrophy and adopting the posture of "sniff," we become deaf and dumb to art's true appeal. To "slop over" is the greatest offence an Englishman can commit. We hold it in such horror that our intellectuals often lose the power to judge what is or is not the adequate expression of feeling. But here again we have extraordinary contradictions. For alongside a considerable posture of "sniff" we have a multitude who wallow in the crudest sentimentalism, an audience for whom it is impossible to lay it on too thick.

Shifting to consideration of sentiment in practical affairs, we shall find a state of things just as muddled. In the Law Courts, for instance, a judge, out of a sentimental regard for marriage, will rebuke counsel for using the expression "this poor woman" of one who, having run away with her husband's brother, tries to atone by committing suicide. "She is a married woman," he says, and to pity her is sentimental. Or an advocate who will appeal in the most sentimental terms to the patriotism of a jury will stigmatise as "sentimental" appeals to feeling in cases of vivisection, wife-beating or other cruelties. Editors, statesmen, preachers, glaringly sentimental in expressing feelings which they think will tell on their audiences, in the same leading articles, speeches, or sermons will condemn the mawkish sentimentality of, say, conscientious objectors, with whose feelings it does not suit their case to agree. The rule in practical life seems to be that your own feeling is sound, and that of your adversary sentimental. The public man sentimentally attached to the idea of Empire or the idea of Progress proclaims the sentimentality of the little Englander or back-to-the-land-man, and honestly supposes himself as much without reproach of sentiment as he is without fear of serious retaliation, since he has behind him a vast bulk of similar sentimentalism. In fact, in life at large you may be sentimental without being called so only when you are on the side of the majority. One does not perhaps exaggerate in saying that we are all sentimentalists; and the difference between us is that most of us safely over-express popular sentiments, and a few of us riskily over-express sentiments which are not popular. Only the latter earn the title "Sentimentalists." Suppose a man to believe after sincere reflection that modern civilisation—with its riot of machinery, scientific experiment, exploitation of the air, and all the concomitant and ever-increasing desires and wants thereby roused in the human animal—has gone for the moment beyond the point of balance, beyond the rule *mens sana in corpore sano;* suppose he seriously considers that under this ever-multiplying taxation on nerve energy and time, under hypnotisation by a blind Progress, men are steadily losing hold on beauty, health, and goodness; that, in fact, his discoveries are being too much for his very moderate digestion, and that he ought for a time to call a halt—just as the individual who is living too fast must take a rest-cure or fall into his trombone—suppose, I say, that a man sincerely believes all this, will he escape being called a sentimentalist? Certainly not, for he is running counter to a sentimentalism much more popular than his own, a sentimentalism which believes in Progress (with a definition of what Progress is left out), talks of the indomitable human spirit, *per ardua ad astra,* and damns the consequences. If he says "More simplicity, fewer wants, home-grown food, not so much rushing about, more true beauty, more time to enjoy it, better instruction in how to enjoy it"—in other words, a normal temperature instead of 102—he is a poor thing in the eyes of those who outnumber him a hundred to one. The point is this: he may be wrong, but he is no more sentimental than they are. And the moral of this and many another possible illustration is: "Before I call a man a sentimentalist, let me look well at myself, at my own feelings and beliefs. I live in a very glass house; I must be careful how I throw stones!"

Sentimentalism, then, whether in life or in literature, is simply a riding before the hounds. Of this we are all guilty at times. But as often as not the charge "sentimentalist" is a mere partisan term of abuse, unfounded in fact; for it is not sentimental to have strong feelings (however eccentric) and to give them adequate, that is to say strong and sincere, expression.

But putting sentimentalism—over-expression—aside, how far is it good that we should be men and women of sentiment—moved, that is, by feeling rather than by calculation, by the heart rather than by the head? Again comes in the question of balance. Amongst people like the English—although a most baffling and contradictory race—one would say that, on the whole, the head predominates. What has been called Anglo-Saxon phlegm or English common-sense rules the roost. For the stability of national life that is probably a blessing. If our judges, our statesmen, our juries were men of feeling, it might not work to our advantage, however much their hard-headedness may annoy us at times. But the mere fact that one may always rely in England on a majority of the common-sensical makes the man or woman of sentiment necessary and valuable among us. And one thing is clear: no amount of trying to be men of feeling can make us into them; we are, or we are not. The ideal, no doubt, is to have heart and head about equally developed—but the ideal is rare, as a search for instances will soon reveal.

Of the American case one hesitates to hazard opinion. Although outstanding instances of the golden mean, such as Lincoln and Lee, are perhaps easier to come by than with us, America would seem to be a naturally excessive country. To an outsider it appears to abound in sentimentalism, to have a formula of over-expression just as we have a formula of under-expression. But, as we have seen, sentimentalism is not sentiment. A man may be sentimental and yet be hard as nails; and America certainly excels in a special brand of hard-headedness. Probably America is in more danger from hard-head than from soft heart.

1922.

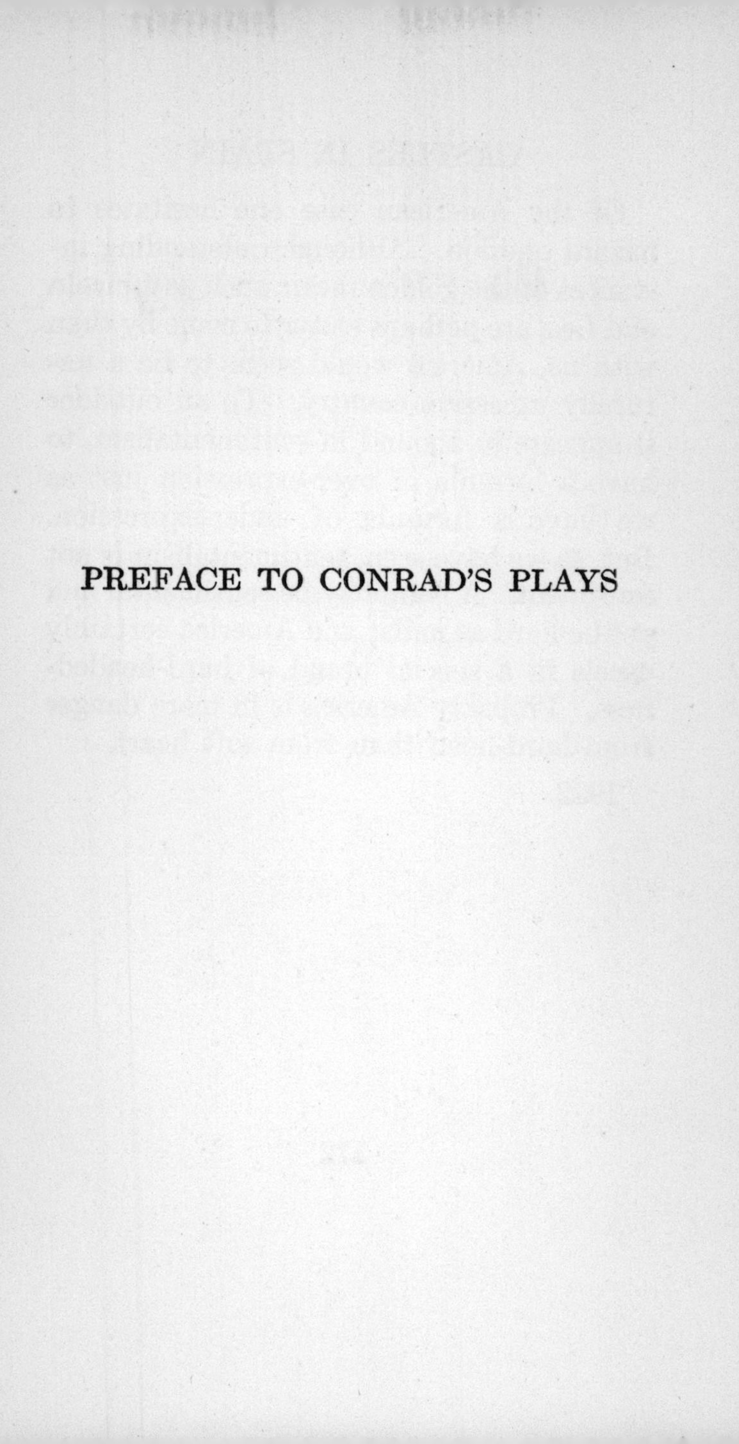

PREFACE TO CONRAD'S PLAYS

PREFACE TO CONRAD'S PLAYS

CONRAD'S three plays, *One Day More*, *Laughing Anne*, and *The Secret Agent* are all adaptations from stories, and the two in this volume have, curiously enough, the same main theme—the suffering of a woman capable of self-sacrifice. The fact that they are adaptations from stories makes it the more difficult to answer the usual speculation whether this great novelist could, if he had given his time to the task, have become a great dramatist—a speculation, indeed, somewhat idle. In a writing life of thirty years a man has time for much variety. We know that Conrad had a keen dramatic sense; we know—at least I know—that he had fitful longings to write for the stage. And the fact that he never, in all those years, wrote directly for it is to me proof that his nature recoiled too definitely from the limitations which the stage imposes on word painting and the subtler efforts of a psychologist. The novel suited his nature better than the play, and he instinctively kept to it. If, through unhappy accident, he had begun by writing for the stage, without having first experienced the wider freedom and tasted the more exquisite savour of the novel, he would probably have become one of the greatest dramatists of our time. But we should have lost by it, for as a novelist he was in many respects unique.

The process of adaptation is, generally, fatal to the achievement of a stage masterpiece; yet in *One Day More* Conrad so nearly achieved a little masterpiece as to show natural aptitude of the highest order.

It is, in some sort, fitting that I should write this little introduction, since that first of his adaptations for the stage was made in my studio workroom on Campden Hill. Conrad worked at one end of it, on *One Day More,* while, at the other end, I was labouring at *The Man of Property*. He sat at a table close to the big window, I stood at a desk with my back to him, and now and then we would stop and exchange lamentations on the miseries of our respective lots.

"My dear fellow," he would say, "this is too horrible for words." Conrad did not suffer from satisfaction with his own work; yet *One Day More* gave him a certain pleasure when he had finished it, and he was eager to see it performed.

He wrote from Capri in May 1905: "Another piece of news is that (would you believe it?) the Stage Society wishes to perform *To-morrow*" (as it was then called) "next June. Colvin wrote me. Several men, and amongst them G. B. Shaw, profess themselves very much struck." They were right to be struck—the little play has a strange and haunting quality, and Old Hagberd, Harry and Bessie are impressive creations.

Not being in England when it was performed, I cannot recall what sort of reception it had from the *cognoscenti* of the Stage Society, but it has evidently been too weird and uncompromising a little piece of tragedy for London Town at large.

I do not know when Conrad adapted *Laughing Anne* from the story *Because of the Dollars,* and indeed never read it till I came to write this preface. Demanding in its short life three scene-sets, none of them easy, and the last exceptionally difficult in stage conditions, it has as yet, I believe, never been performed. It exemplifies that kind of innocence which novelists commonly have as to what will "go down" on the stage. Conrad probably never realised that a "man without hands" would be an almost unbearable spectacle; that what you can write about freely cannot always be endured by the living eye. Anyone who has passed over the Bridge of Galata in the old days—which, very likely, are the new days too—and seen what the beggars there offered to one's sense of pity, will appreciate the nausea inspired by that particular deformity. The lighting, too, of the last scene would be most difficult—effects that depend on shudderings grounded in dim light are to be avoided. A moment or two —yes; but a whole scene—no! To read this play, however, is a pleasure. The figures of Davidson, of poor Laughing Anne, of Fector, Bamtz, and the monster without hands, are thoroughly effective; and, except for those physical drawbacks, the play is admirably contrived.

I am tempted to refer here to the longer adaptation of that most impressive novel, *The Secret Agent;* for we have therein a salient illustration, not only of the difficulty of adaptation, but of the fundamental difference between novel and drama as a medium for presenting life. *The Secret Agent* was a novel of atmosphere, a revelation of hidden depths in human nature, and a sort of creation of an underworld. It depended for its triumph on innumerable subtleties, and the fidelity of a sustained mood. Those of us, not many, who work in both forms know, to a degree not possible, perhaps, to those who work in one, or work in neither, the cruel obstacles which the physical conditions of the stage put in the way of the sustained mood. I would say that the stage, as a faithful vehicle of mood, falls as far short of the novel as the cinema falls short of the stage. All art admittedly depends on craft, on the sort of devising which we call technique; even the novel, that most liberal and elastic medium, has its own severities, makes its own rigorous demands on ingenuity, dramatic instinct, and selective power—but they are difficulties to be overcome in a strict privacy by the writer steeped in his mood, camped on his theme without interference. In writing for the stage the cramp of a hundred and one extra influences comes into play, device becomes trick work, selection is dictated to by physical conditions beyond control. The confirmed novelist, accustomed to freedom and his own conscience, is often given to impatience, and a measure of contempt towards even his own writing for the stage. That merely means, as a rule, that he does not realise the basic difference between the two forms. And, however good a novelist such an one may be, he will inevitably be a less good dramatist. A form must "enthuse" one, as the Americans say, before one can do it justice. One cannot approach the stage successfully without profound respect and a deep recognition that its conditions are the essentials of an appeal totally distinct from that of the novel.

I do not think that Conrad was ignorant of this—not at all. His shortcomings were due, partly, to the almost insuperable difficulties of adaptation and, partly, to inadequate mastery of trick work which has to be learned. In other words, he had not given enough time to the dramatic form. He did not quite know how to balance his effects, how to economise his words, or how to keep his line of action clear and inevitable. A little more experience would have shown him, for instance, that the salon scene, as written, in his dramatic version of *The Secret Agent* was dead wood.

I read his adaptation in manuscript before the play was produced, and, in answer to my somewhat critical letter, received one which contained this passage:

"The play is purely illustrative. It is because of that" (illustrative) "nature that I have let it spread itself into scenes which from the point of action alone may, and obviously do, appear superfluous and detached from the subject. Whereas to my feeling they are all closely to the point."

This is Conrad's defence of the play as it stands. It does not go quite to the root of the matter, for as much feeling and illustrative value as he put into the play would have been preserved, and could even have been increased, by the elimination of *longueurs,* if his technique had been equal to the task; in other words, if he had given some of the years he gave to the novel to writing drama instead. And, anyway, the mood and illustrative value of his theme did not and could not receive as full expression in the play as it did in the novel.

So that it comes back to this: one is glad

he didn't give time enough to play-writing. Those of us who remember that amazing cab drive in the novel—the gem passage in *The Secret Agent*—unrenderable on the stage, realise very well that his time was better concentrated on an unfettered fidelity to his moods in his unflinching scrutiny of men and things, on his power of painting in words, and on a psychological insight unsurpassed for depth and subtlety.

Of the actual production of *The Secret Agent*, which I thought left much to be desired, Conrad wrote with his characteristic generosity:

"Now it is all over, my state may be described as that of serene joy, only marred by remorse at the injustice of my past thoughts towards the actors, who had a lot of characters certainly not of a 'stock' kind thrown at their heads just twenty days before the first performance. Now, like a man touched by grace, I think of them with actual tenderness and almost with affection. . . .

"The disagreeable part of this business is to see wasted the hard work of people who depend on it for their livelihood, and for whom success would mean assured employment and ease of mind. One feels guilty somehow."

There spoke the heart of Conrad, for ever in sympathy with men and women who did their job as well as they could, and thinking of others before himself.

1924.

BURNING LEAVES

BURNING LEAVES

WHEN autumn comes, and leaves are gathered into little heaps and slow fire set to them, all who have passed the meridian of life are moved by the acrid odour and the trailing blue of the smoke, as if they saw and scented the leafage of their own pasts burning—leafage which was green and smelled of lemons when it burst from the bud. A town-scent—this of burning leaves, whose nearest parallel in the country is the scent of rotting leaves; not so strong or provocative of melancholy, perhaps because the uncleared leaves are going naturally back to the mould from which the trees have drawn their life; or, perhaps—a less literary reason—because the scent from rotting leaves is so much milder i' the nostril. All primitive inevitability—birth, coupling, death—takes a larger place, and yet is less poignant and startling in the country than in towns.

Out in the open we are framed in the unceasing process of Nature, among plants and birds and animals; in towns bound in mechanical conspiracy to conceal that process; we burn our leaves, and remove the sight of their long decay; we compress slow emotion into swift feeling.

Curious, by the way, that we should have a prayer against sudden death; and if our Litany were to be revised, suffrage would convert it. Most of us would now prefer to have our lives blown out as a man blows out a candle; choose to burn steadily to a swift last, instead of with a flickering sorrowful dwindling of our flames into darkness that we can see creeping round us. "To sudden death, not premature, O Fate, deliver us!" would run our prayer. There has ever been something mean, too, about a preparation for dying, with its calculated confession of wrong living, and its squirming effort to square accounts at the last; as if a man, having comfortably cheated his neighbours all his life, sought the odour of honesty only when mortal sickness deprives him of the power of cheating them any more. A singular cynicism or a strange lack of charity in estimating the Divine Character attends the notion of a "deathbed repentance."

But when we smell burning leaves we do not remember our murky thoughts and actions; the mouldering heaps are golden, the smoke therefrom the colour of happiness, its scent sharp-sweet. Relish in past experience—even painful experience, regret for experience spent and absent now, is what moves him or her who watches and sniffs that smoke.

A pity that we cannot see, slow-forming before our eyes, the ghost trees of our past lives, their trunks and spine branches of development, with all our sensations budding, living, fluttering upon them, see our every action, thought and feeling spread in the pattern of their growth towards the top where leaves are already few. Self-growth is hard to comprehend in its slow and imperceptible transformations. The children we were are frankly unrecognisable by ourselves at fifty. Our spiritual and bodily metabolism, so probably one and the same thing, is beyond our powers of tracing out; but scenting the trailed smoke of burning leaves we come perhaps nearer than at any other time to appreciation of how we stretch back year on year to innocence in a holland suit.

"Oh! the long days in the distance enchanted!" piled in that heap, they exhale their burnt incense, no flame visible; it trails away thin and blue towards where the sunset is preparing. Lives! What invisible runners they are!

1923.

AFTER SEEING A PLAY IN 1903

AFTER SEEING A PLAY IN 1903

IN every man feeling and common-sense are at each other's throats; life is the see-saw of these two forces, and no single mortal sits upon the centre of its gravity, for none could endure the unutterable dullness of that sacred post.

Our attitudes, our actions, and our thoughts—academic or contemporary, soft or hard, material or ideal—are the outcome of this eternal struggle, and if every man examined deep enough into his own conduct, which Heaven forbid, he would be astonished to find that it all depended on his private performance of this great tragic-comic see-saw act.

And so it comes about that mankind is divided into men of heart and men of head. But we in England, with our national sense of fair play, find no fun in a contest of balance between an ostrich's egg and a bantam's, especially when the latter is addled, being composed almost entirely of vagabonds, Irishmen, and artists. We are nearly all men of head—of common-sense, and when we see an Irishman sacrifice his dinner to a witty remark, a vagabond go without work for the sake of his liberty, and an artist write a play for the interior of his desk, we are not bitter, nor angry; we pity them, because we see them yielding to the prompting of a mysterious desire, the satisfaction of a sensation-craving nerve of which we ourselves are guiltless, and because we know that they are in a fitting and crushing minority.

It is this apt and proper disproportion within us between common-sense and feeling which has produced the masterpieces of our greater modern dramatists. They recognise that men were made for morality and not morality made by men, and that the paramount duty of the playwright is to convey the triumph of the preconceived notion of things in preference to showing the forces of Nature acting and reacting upon human beings; and they give us, week after week and year after year, works which precisely fulfil the requirements of the preponderant common-sense in the body politic, crown and set a seal on that common-sense itself, exalt it to the stars, and bless it with complacency. For our greater modern dramatists are all men of head, men of common-sense, believing to the full in the folly of the artist and the gloom of the interior of desks.

In a poll taken among the public which crowded with me to witness the play from which I have just come, ninety would record that the finest, the most tremendous moments of it are the hero's fourth act rhetorics and the heroine's renunciation, and only ten would absurdly maintain that her "Oh! Mr.——!" when he kisses her in the first act, and her waltz on the roof to the barrel-organ, are worth all the rest of the play put together. For in that "Oh! Mr.——!", in that waltz on the roof, there is all the craving for love, for pleasure, for light, for colour that lies deep and dark at the bottom of each human heart—in other words, they give the human heart away; and that is too dangerous, in a life fundamentally connected with daily bread.

Let us examine a little the way in which these chief characters falsify themselves at crucial points in conformity with the paramount demands of common-sense, or shall we call it—of morality? We assume that they are intended for serious creations, even for types; and start with the hero. Now the hero—a serious creation—is the type of the morally rotten man who if he does not stand for rottenness stands for nothing, and of whose moral rottenness we are constantly assured by others and by himself. This hero pursues a young girl in a way which induces us to believe that he is passionately in love with her. In the fourth act, after being placed in a position to carry his point, he is caused to refrain, and forces us to conclude either that he does not after all stand for rottenness, in which case he stands for nothing, or that, in his abstention, he has made a bow to those of us who cannot tolerate the thought that the heroine should lose her virtue and the chance of marrying a man she does not love. It will be said that in life we do not always follow the main trend of our characters, but surely we should not be honouring our greater modern dramatists if we supposed them ignorant of their duty to put their characters into positions from which they can only issue by following the main trend of their natures.

We watch, moreover, the uneasiness which dogs the hero throughout this play, the virtuous and carking consciousness that he is rotten; but is this self-condemnation ever really present in the human animal? Let us take those of our acquaintances who are on his plane and search the impression they have made upon us. If, and I think it not improbable, we find that they all seem to act and think with a sort of poetic justice and conviction of their own, as if they actually had separate lives with separate and to them quite justifying motives and phenomena—if we find this, we are bound once more to recognise the graceful bow of our dramatist and his creation to our common-sense and our morality.

Now let us take the case of the heroine. She again is a serious creation, a type, and to decide of what she is a type we go to those moments when she gave away the human heart. She is the type—I think she has been so described—of the affectionate, weak, and naturally pleasure-loving girl; and we are taken through a variety of situations which have no purpose but to show us the harmless instability of this poor little shuttlecock in the cross-currents of life. At last we come to what has been termed the "great scene" in the fourth act, and suddenly we discover that the heroine, brought face to face with what shocks our common-sense, cuts herself away in a flutter of firmness, and sets at naught that conception of herself which she had been at such pains to instil into our minds. Flattered and soothed that she should have acted in a strictly sensible manner, we yet feel a little uneasy, and some of us, more cantankerous than the rest, ask: Why take the trouble to draw a weak character if in the only situation that matters you make her strong? And if it be answered that her "strength" in the fourth act is really weakness—just anæmia—then why that spurious flavour of strength, why the "virtue rewarded" of the epilogue?

No! There it is! However you look at it, the hero and the heroine must never go beyond what will come all right, never exceed the standard of what our common-sense dictates: they must keep an infallible and wary eye upon their position in Society; and from their births are destined to a moral end.

And this brings us once more to the charming unanimity which exists between the greater modern dramatists and ourselves. Permeated through and through with common-sense, neither they nor we can bear that the human heart should be given away; we cannot attend to that "Oh! Mr.——!", to that waltz upon the roof; we must have our rhetorics and our renunciations.

Men of heart and men of head! Not until we reverse the proportion between these two, not till the moon has shone by day, will our greater modern dramatists believe that the principal things in life are neither marriage nor a position in society, but love and death; that art is rooted in feeling; that inevitability has a certain value; and that the only epic virtue is courage.

1903.

SIX NOVELISTS IN PROFILE

AN ADDRESS

SIX NOVELISTS IN PROFILE

AN ADDRESS

MY first profile is that of Charles Dickens, who, born in London in 1812, died at Gadshill in 1870. In that early and in some sort great Victorian Age, English novelists—in spite of much generous revolt against particular social evils—solemnly accepted the conventions, morals, standards, ideals, and enterprises of their day; believed with all their hearts that life was worth living; regarded its current values as absolute; had no ironic misgivings, nor any sense that existence is a tragi-comedy. They saw no grin on the face of Fate. They were almost majestically unselfconscious. Dickens was a true child of his age.

Shakespeare, two hundred and fifty years earlier, was much more introspective and philosophical.

Dickens was an extraordinarily artless writer, he let his genius run where and when it would; the perfect master of happy extravagance; a natural stylist of extraordinary force, he was a born teller of a tale, with amazing knowledge of human nature and human types; a great imaginative creator, with the zest of a school-boy at a Christmas feast.

He was an enemy of "humbug," fiercely resentful of cruelty, intolerance, and solemn stupidity, and his writing life was a long attack on the social evils he came across. He lashed officialism, hypocrisy, and the abuse of power. But in spite of this disposition towards satire, he makes us think always first of the story and the characters. All his spontaneous, crude, richly creative work is coloured with an eager, broad humanity. "All kind things," he once said, "must be done on their own account, and for their own sake, and without the least reference to gratitude."

Probably Dickens, like most novelists, accounted himself a poet. But there is little evidence to support this accusation. There was in him no paganism, no influence by Greek or Latin culture; no trace of any foreign influence whatever; he was English of the English, and from no other writings can England be so well comprehended even now. If some of his characters were little more than names attached to extravagant attitudes of conduct, they show his genius the more in that we accept them as men and women. He had the persuasiveness of great vitality; he wrote with a fine "gusto." In the pages of Dickens virtue is virtue, vice is vice, seldom "the twain do meet" in the way they meet in all—except our public men. He paints the ethical with a glaring brush; we should charge at the picture as bulls at red if there were any pretence of art about it. But in those days our novelists did not bother about art. The literary gatherings of that period in England confined themselves, I suspect, to jesting, drink, politics, and oysters. Dickens's great contemporary, Thackeray, indeed, had heard of art, and thought it worthy of a certain patronage; Dickens himself identified it, I fear, with foreigners, and showed it the back door. He was robust, but it is strange to think of him writing as he did when, not two hundred miles away, such an accomplished artist as Prosper Merimée was writing *Carmen* and *The Venus d'Ille*, Turgenev was writing *Smoke* and *Torrents of Spring*, and across the Atlantic Nathaniel Hawthorne *The Scarlet Letter* and Edgar Poe his *Strange Tales*. No one would dream of going to Dickens to learn consciously the art of novel-writing; yet all can draw from him subconsciously the foundation of phrase, for he was a born writer, and the foundation of philosophy, though he was no philosopher.

Beyond dispute, he is, to me, the greatest English novelist, and the greatest example in the annals of all novel-writing of the triumph of sheer exuberant genius. By native imagination and force of expression he has left human nature imprinted on men's minds more variously and vividly than any other Western novelist.

Culture does not teach one to write novels.

Education in the technical sense serves rather to choke than to encourage the power of imagination. Before I began to write novels I had forgotten nearly all I learned at school and college. Precise scholars are rarely imaginative writers of any force, they know too much and too little. The vividly imaginative seldom have relish for the exact study of anything except—life. Feeling for the colour and rhythm of words may be helped by reading poetry and fine prose, but it is due more to inborn sensibility and a musical ear. The power of construction also is inborn. The power of poignant expression is inborn; it cannot be acquired, it can only be improved. Nor can anyone teach an imaginative writer to feel or see life in any particular way. After he has learned to read and write, a novelist can be taught by others only how *not* to write; his true schoolmaster is life itself.

Now, when, as we are all fond of doing, we use the word art in relation to the novel, we have to remember the novel's history;

the variety of forms through which it has passed and is still passing since Cervantes and that first great Western novel, *Don Quixote.*

The early novels of all Western countries took a picaresque form; they were strings of biographical incident loosely joined by the thread of one or more central figures, rather like a string of onions and often with something of their savour. Unity and proportion, except of this crude nature, were not thought of. The novel had length but neither breadth nor roundness. Towards the beginning of the nineteenth century, one can see the novel growing rounder and rounder until, when Dickens wrote, the egg was, roughly speaking, its recognised shape—plethoric in the middle and skimpy at both ends, like a successful novelist. What conditioned this gradual change I cannot say, but the development was rather like that which we observe in painting at the time of the Renaissance. Under Jane Austen, Dickens, Balzac, Stendhal, Scott, Dumas, Thackeray and Hugo, the novel attained a certain relation of part to whole; but it was left for one of more poetic feeling and greater sensibility than any of these to perfect its proportions, and introduce the principle of selection, until there was that complete relation of part to whole which goes to the making of what we call a work of art. This writer was Turgenev, as supreme in the art of the novel as Dickens was artless.

Ivan Turgenev, born at Orel in Russia in 1818, died at Bougival near Paris in 1883. Critics have usually been preoccupied by his detachment from his native Russian culture, by his variation from the loose-jointed giant Gogol, and the shapeless giant Dostoievsky. Anxiously calling him a Westerner, they have omitted to notice that the West did not influence him so much as he influenced the West. Turgenev achieved his unique position from within himself; he was the finest natural poet who ever wrote novels. It was *that* which separated him from his great Russian contemporaries, and gave him his distinction and his influence in the West. Russia did not like Turgenev—he had a bad habit. He told the truth. No country likes that. It is considered especially improper in novelists. Russia got rid of him. But if he had never left Russia his work would still have taken the shape it did—because of his instinctive feeling for form. He had a perfect sense of "line"; moulding and rounding his themes within himself before working them out in written words; and, though he never neglected the objective, he thought in terms of atmosphere rather than in terms of fact. Turgenev, an aristocrat, a man of culture, susceptible to the impression of foreign literatures, devoted to music and painting, a reader and writer of plays and poems, touches Dickens only at three broad but all-important points: the intense understanding they both had of human nature, the intense interest they both took in life, the intense hatred they both felt for cruelty and humbug. Let those who doubt the truth of this last resemblance read Turgenev's little story

Mumu, about the dog of the dumb serf porter Gerasim. No more stirring protest against tyrannical cruelty was ever penned in terms of art. Dickens was the least fastidious of writers, Turgenev one of the most fastidious. Dickens attacked a cruelty, an abuse, an extravagance, directly or by way of frank caricature; Turgenev sank his criticism in objective terms of portraiture. His style in Russian, we are told, is exquisite; even in translations much of its charm and essential flavour lingers. His dialogue is easy, interesting, life-like, yet always significant and revealing; his characters serve the main theme or idea with which he is dealing, but never fail to be real men and women too. His descriptions of Nature are delightful. *Byezhin Prairie, A Tryst, Torrents of Spring* haunt one with their beauty. The whole of his work is saturated in the half-melancholy rapture which Nature stirs in a poetic temperament. In his definite prose-poems he was much less of a poet than in his sketches and novels, because self-consciousness destroys true poetry, which is the springing forth of mood and feeling almost in spite of self. In Turgenev there is a slight survival of burlesque, a dash of the grotesque, a suspicion of what we should call "the old-fashioned"; but considering that he was in his prime sixty years ago how marvellously little the machine of his art creaks!

The English novel, though on the whole perhaps more varied and rich than that of any other country, has—from *Clarissa Harlowe* down to *Ulysses*—been inclined to self-indulgence; it often goes to bed drunk. And it owes to Turgenev more than to anyone what niceness of deportment and proportion it now has. I, at least, acknowledge a great debt. To him and to de Maupassant I served that spiritual and technical apprenticeship which every young writer serves, guided by some deep kinship in spirit to one or other of the old past-masters of his craft. Flaubert, the apostle of self-conscious artistry, never had quite the vital influence that Turgenev exercised on English writers; a certain feeling of enclosure clings about his work, an indoor atmosphere. Against Turgenev that was never charged, not even when, about the year 1907, it became a literary fashion in England to disparage him, because certain of our critics had discovered—rather late, perhaps—a new Russian lamp in Dostoievsky. There was room, one might have thought, for the two lights; but in the literary world it is difficult to light a new lamp without putting out an old one. That is now ancient history, and Turgenev has recovered his name, but not his influence. He is too balanced, and too essentially poetic, for the new age.

And so I come to my third profile—that of one who, I am told by some, is still read in his native France, and who, I am told by others, has been laid on the shelf. The great literary achievements of Guy de Maupassant, born in 1850 and dying in 1893, were crowded into a space of but twelve years. His name is popularly associated with the short story, but his full measure, to my thinking, can only be taken through his novels, and tales of medium length like *Boule de Suif* and *Yvette.* All his work, long or short, tragic or trivial, is dramatic in essence; and, though he wrote but little for the theatre, he was richly endowed with the qualities that make a great dramatist. In the essentials of style, he is the prince of teachers. The vigour of his vision, and his thought, the economy and clarity of the expression in which he clothed them, have not yet been surpassed. Better than any other writer, he has taught us what to leave out; better than any illustrated for us Flaubert's maxim: "Study an object till its essential difference from every other is perceived and can be rendered in words." His work forms a standing rebuke to the confusion, the shallow expressionism, the formless egoism which are not infrequently taken for art. But though disciplined to the finger-nails as a craftsman, he reached and displayed the depths of human feeling. His sardonic nature hated prejudice and stupidity, had in it a vein of deep and indignant pity, a burning curiosity, piercing vision, and a sensitiveness seldom equalled. He was well equipped for the rendering of life.

At times he wrote stories unworthy of him. At times his work smelled of the lamp. And the mental breakdown which clouded the end of his life left a searing mark on some of his later tales. But in spite of these defects, I follow the dictum of Tolstoi in placing Maupassant above his master Flaubert, both in style and temperamental gifts.

In Maupassant we reach, as it were, the apex of the shaped story, the high mark of fiction which knows exactly what it is about, and has for aim, through the objective method, revelation of the strange depths and shallows of human nature. A form of art highly disciplined and detached where the temperament of the author is allowed freedom only in the range of subject and character selected. In England Maupassant was once looked on as a ferocious realist; to literary youth he is now a rosy-fingered, pinafored romanticist, and his form considered too set, finished, and dramatic. Forgive, then, this quotation from his preface to *Pierre et Jean*:

"En somme, le public est composé de groupes nombreux qui nous crient: 'Consolez-moi.' 'Amusez-moi.' 'Attristez-moi.' 'Attendrissez-moi.' 'Faites-moi rêver.' 'Faites-moi rire.' 'Faites-moi frémir.' 'Faites-moi pleurer.' 'Faites-moi penser.' Seuls, quelques esprits d'élite demandent a l'artiste: Faites-moi quelque chose de beau, dans la forme qui vous conviendra le mieux, suivant votre tempérament. L'artiste essaie, reuissit ou échoue."

His ideal was to make a beautiful thing following his temperament. Since endless controversy rages over the word "beauty," I shall be forgiven for not plunging into it. But the artist who creates what is living and true has achieved beauty also, in my considered opinion. De Maupassant made many a capture of the shy bird Beauty.

It is curious to think that Tolstoi, whose profile is so different, admired him. Born in 1828 at Yasnaya Polyana in Russia, and dying in 1910 at Astaporo, Leo Tolstoi began to write when he was twenty-four years old, after a full and energetic youth. *Tales of Sevastopol,* written during the Crimean War, in which he served in the Russian army, brought him instant celebrity. His chief masterpieces, *War and Peace* and *Anna Karenina,* were written between 1864 and 1873.

Tolstoi is a fascinating puzzle. So singular an instance of artist and reformer rolled into one frame is not, I think, elsewhere to be found. The preacher in him, who took such charge of his later years, was already casting a shadow over the artist-writer of *Anna Karenina.* There is even an indication of the moralist in the last part of that tremendous novel *War and Peace.*

About his work, in fact, is an ever-present sense of spiritual duality. It is a battlefield on which we watch the ebb and flow of unending conflict, the throb and stress of a gigantic disharmony. Explanation of this mysterious quality must be left to the doctors now that our personalities are controlled by our glands; so that if we have plenty of pituitary, we are artists; and too little adrenal, perhaps, moralists.

In choosing a single novel to label with those words so dear to the confectioners of symposiums—"the greatest ever written"—I would select *War and Peace.* In it Tolstoi rides two themes, like a circus rider on his two piebald horses, and by a miracle reaches the stable door still mounted and still whole. The secret of his triumph lies in the sheer interest with which his creative energy has invested every passage. The book is six times as long as an ordinary novel, but it never flags, never wearies the reader, and the ground—of human interest and historical event, of social life and national life—covered in it is prodigious.

Tolstoi's method, in this novel as in all his work, is cumulative—the method of an infinity of fact and pictorial detail; the opposite of Turgenev's, who relied on selection and concentration, on atmosphere, and poetic balance. Tolstoi fills in all the spaces, and leaves little to the imagination; but with such vigour, such freshness, that it is all interesting. His "style" in the narrow sense is by no means remarkable; all his work bears the impress of a mind more concerned with the thing said than with the way in which to say it.

But if one may add to innumerable definitions: Style is the power in a writer to remove all barriers between himself and his reader—the triumph of style is the creation of intimacy. Then, though such a definition puts many stylists out of court, it leaves Tolstoi a stylist of mark, for no author, in his story-telling, produces a more intimate feeling of actual life. He is free, in fact, from the literary self-consciousness which so often spoils the work of polished writers. Tolstoi was carried away by his impulses, whether creative or reformative. He never stood on the shores of streams trying first one foot and then the other—that pet vice of modern art. Art, when it has life and meaning, comes from an artist possessed by his theme. The rest of art is just exercise in technique, which helps artists to render the greater impulses when they come—too seldom. The painter who spends half his life agonising over what he ought to be—Post-Impressionist, Cubist, Futurist, Expressionist, Dadaist, paulopost-Dadaist, or whatever they are by now—who is ever developing a new and wonderful technique and changing his æsthetic outlook, does work which, like his mood, is self-conscious and tentative. But when a theme seizes on him all doubts about expression are resolved, and a master's work is wrought.

Tolstoi knew his Russian land and the Russian peasant as well, perhaps, as an aristocrat could know them; but he is not so close to the soul and body of Russia as Tchehov, who came of the people, and knew them from inside. The Russia of Tolstoi's great novels, *War and Peace* and *Anna Karenina,* is now a Russia of the past, perhaps only the crust of that Russia of the past—split and crumbled beyond repair. We are fortunate to have those two great pictures of a vanished fabric.

I pass to my fifth profile—that of Conrad.

Jospeh Conrad Korzeniowski, born in 1857 of Polish gentry who suffered in the rebellion of 1863, shared as a child his parents' exile, spent his boyhood in Russian Poland, his early manhood in adventure, and became an officer in British sailing ships, laying up strange store of thought, tradition, life, and language. He gave up the sea for literature, some thirty years ago, became naturalized in England, and began authorship under the name of Joseph Conrad. His twenty odd volumes of fiction, in a language not native to him, with a quality of style so rich and varied, form an unique achievement in the history of literature. The bewildering colour and imagery of his early works were toned with the years to a more sober texture; but, taking his work as a whole, no writer of English has exceeded him in sheer power of word-painting. His handling of design was not impeccable. Essentially colourist, essentially "raconteur," he had a way of folding his story over and over itself, which gave indeed a peculiar subtlety, richness, and depth to its psychology and atmosphere, but left one wandering at times in the mazes of a sub-tropical forest without much hope of ever getting out. And yet in the end one would come again to the daylight of open country, and the conclusion of what Conrad himself called "a moral discovery." Conrad had, beyond all novelists, the cosmic sense. Throughout the long drama of his work, Fate, powerful and mysterious, plays the star part; his human beings, though highly individualised, perform the minor rôles. And from this subordination they derive a pathos and poignancy, an epic quality which attaches to those who struggle to the death against that which must beat them in the end. This feeling that Nature is first, Man second—even when he preserves his moral integrity and puts up a great fight, as he often does in Conrad's novels—this feeling is not forced on the reader by conscious effort, it reaches to him in subtle ways, from the temperament of the novelist.

The cosmic sense is rare. We are most of us too definitely anthropomorphic to have it; we see even the Deity from the human point of view; have little of the old Greek sense of our position in the scheme of things. *L'état c'est nous.* We *are* the scheme and the working thereof. This may be natural, but from the point of view of Father Time, who for some billions of years looked on a world untenanted by human beings, it is rather a parvenu conviction. Mystery enwraps the cause, the origin, the end of life, yea, even of human life. And acceptance of that mystery brings a certain dignity to existence, the kind of dignity we find in the work of Conrad.

The refinements of psychology, of motive and feeling, are carried by Conrad to a pitch only surpassed in English literature, perhaps, by Henry James, and they were neither of them English. But there is a complete difference between the emotional conception of these two writers. Henry James drank tea—Conrad wine—speaking metaphorically. Henry James lived imaginatively in a world from which elemental nature and the primitive raw material of human nature were excluded. None of his characters are permitted to indulge in crude or violent feelings; the human intellect is the hub round which their scheme of things revolves. Conrad lived imaginatively in a world from which nothing was excluded, not even savagery, and where elemental nature, with its thoroughly bad manners, generally formed one if not two of the party.

The fascination of his writing lies in a singular blending of reality with romance—he paints a world of strange skies and seas, rivers, forests, men, strange harbours and ships, all, to our tamed understanding, touched a little by the marvellous. Beyond all modern writers he had lived romance; lived it for many years with a full unconscious pulse, the zest of a young man loving adventure, and before ever he thought to become a writer. How many talents among us are spoiled by having no store of experience and feeling, *unconsciously* amassed, to feed on! How many writers, without cream inside the churn, are turning out butter!

To peoples who have the sea in their blood, like the English, the appeal of Conrad is the greater. With the exception of Herman Melville in *The White Whale,* and Pierre Loti in *Pêcheurs d'Islande,* no novelist has so rendered the moods, the fascination, the menace of the sea. His writing of it is touched with awe and coloured by the inexhaustible interest of a man who has fought with and overcome or yielded to its infinite variety. *The Nigger of the Narcissus, Typhoon,* and *Youth* are masterpieces indeed.

Passing from Conrad to the last of my profiles is to turn from Malay shores to the Quai d' Orléans. In life's drama Conrad was on the stage, Anatole France, from his birth in 1844 to his death in 1924, sat in the stalls. His was the detached and learned mind. A pure bookman, bred and born in the centre of bookish knowledge, he was erudite as few men have been, and withal—a scourge. His whip was the most elegant and perhaps the most effective ever wielded. He destroyed with a suavity that has never been excelled. He perforated prejudice and punctured idolatry so adroitly that the ventilation holes were scarcely visible, and the victims felt draughts without knowing why. In his long writing career—he began in 1868 and was still writing at his death in 1924—he only thrice, if I am not mistaken, assumed the rôle of novelist pure. *Le Crime de Sylvestre Bonnard, Le Lys Rouge* and *L'Histoire Comique* stand out in method from his other work. In theme alone is he chiefly student of human character and teller of a tale. In his other books he is first the philosopher and satirist. Even a work of art so remarkable as *Thaïs,* a perfect piece of recreation, is in essence critical, and was forged out of a satiric heart. The Bergeret series, though they contain many admirable portraits, was the work of one preoccupied with riddling the prejudices rather than painting the features of human beings. The short masterpiece *Le Procurateur de Judée* presents an unforgettable effigy of Pontius Pilate, but it was written to clothe in perfection a satiric thought. Poor "Crainquebille" is a very human figure, yet it is rather as a walking indictment of human justice that we cherish and remember him. Even little dog Riquet conveys his tail-fluttering criticism of human habits. Anatole France was a subtle and deadly fencer, rather than a trenchant swordsman like Voltaire; his victims still don't know that they are dead. They read him yet, and call him *maître*. Unsurpassed for lucidity and supple elegance, his style was the poetry of pure reason. He was very French. We shall never perhaps see again so perfect an incarnation of the witty French spirit. Not without justification did he take the *nom de plume* of France. His—like all the others in this little gallery—was the profile of a humanist, the most convinced and proselytising of them all. Born fortunately too late for the glory of being burned or beheaded, he succeeded in being excommunicated by the Vatican. Whether the pity which informed the greater part of his writings was the pity of feeling or of reason must be left to those who knew him personally; the urbanity and craft of its expression inclines one who did not know him to suspect the latter. His love, too, of wrapping his indictments in delicate robes of embroidered allegory has to some extent preserved him from attack by those whose creed is: "Say nothing that means anything, and be long about it." Excommunication by fashion is a glory he has not yet entirely achieved, though in certain Parisian coteries, and among the weaker-minded in New York, to admire him would be risky. One may say with certainty that he recoiled from cruelty, narrowness, excess, and crudity—Monsieur Bergeret was his spirit without its sting, an intensely civilised being, incapable of life outside the ring of culture—Anatole France in the Malay seas, in the fields of Russia, in the purlieus of Victorian London, among Normandy peasants, is—unthinkable. He excelled in the ironic mingling of values. *Le Jongleur de Notre Dame*—how tender his irony could be! Loving the pagan, he yet seems to have reverenced the heart of the Sermon on the Mount, for *Heureux les Simples* is the moral of many of his tales. His villagers might set up the Virgin in gold and in ivory—but she ever fell down till they set her up in plain wood. He revelled in shredding away from the core of Christianity with his thin chased knife all pretences, shams, and superstitions. One reads *Crainquebille* and knows that injustice was anathema to his spirit. *L'Affaire Dreyfus* brought Anatole France out of the groves of his philosophic fancy, and *L'Anneau d'Amethyste* was a contribution to Justice almost as potent as Zola's *J'Accuse*. Though a declared Socialist, latterly of an extreme type, he failed, as is usual with men of letters, to influence politics. His direct indulgence in political propaganda stirred no waters. But his diffused and temperamental criticism has cleared away much superstition and deeply affected modern thought.

Is one wrong in feeling that the goose "Modernity" is being cooked—modernity in the sense of the spirit that makes of us *petits maîtres* trying for startling expression of the trivial, for word-patterns unrelated to thought value, for the jazzy music of restive spirits? Is one misled in believing that we are settling back into sober craftsmanship, with a disposition to look askance at the antics of our egos? Or is that wish mother to the thought? One would not deny to the fine bird Modernity some value, now that it is approaching the table. Given the war—it was an inevitable bird. From time to time these explosive periods occur. The spirit walks forth upon the waters, calling out to all to behold it, and, suddenly, with a squeak of surprise, disappears, leaving indeed a few ripples. In literature there is never really stagnation; the main current is all the time unobtrusively flowing on. The antics and splashings on the surface are sometimes excessive, sometimes scarcely visible. They are mostly made by little fish, for the big swim in their element with a certain concentration of purpose. You will have noticed how in painting movement succeeds movement, gets labelled, and becomes old-fashioned, leaving alive this master or that, around whom many had splashed and gambolled—a Turner, a Manet, a Millet, a Whistler, a Gauguin. So is it with Literature, and Time alone assesses the great surviving figures. Form is ever being subtly modified and changed, but it never really leaps. Reaction sees to that. No less than Life is Art organic, and the greater the artist the more he keeps to the main stream, and the natural rate of progression; the less he rushes and gushes or gets into backwaters and splashes away the summer's afternoon.

Art, even the art of the novel, has always been the subject of a "tug-of-war" between two schools of thought—the school that demands of it a revelation or criticism of life, and the school that asks of it nothing but pleasure-giving invention. Both schools, however, in the heat of their struggle for the possession of art tend to forget that, whether a work of art be critical and revealing, or a bit of decorative invention, its essence—that which makes it a work of art—is the presence of the mysterious quality called "life." And the conditions of "life" are: a sufficient relation of part to whole, and a sufficient flavouring of the artist's temperament. For only these elements give to a piece of work the essential novelty of a living thing.

A true work of art remains beautiful and living, though an ebb tide of fashion may leave it for the moment high and dry on the beach. It remains beautiful and living, simply because it has a life of its own. It may be a revelation of nature and human nature, like a drama of Euripides or a novel of Turgenev, or a bit of perfect fantasy like an Andersen fairy-tale, or a *Midsummer Night's Dream*—of such we do not think in terms of fashion.

The conflict, then, ever raging, whether

or no a novelist's work should afford a criticism of life, is idle. Novelists run—as we say—in all shapes. De Maupassant, Turgenev, Conrad have been esteemed pure artists; Dickens, Tolstoi, France certainly have strong veins of the satirist or preacher in them. No one will deny the title "great novelist" to any one of the six; nor has the work of the three "pure artists" been devoid of critical value. Far from it. The fact is that all these six great novelists rendered life in terms of their own temperaments, and no novelist of their range and power of expression fails to be a critic of life. Even Flaubert, apostle of objectivity, æsthetic demi-god, passed profound criticism on life in his masterpieces *Un Cœur Simple, St. Julien l'Hospitalier,* and *Madame Bovary.* Whether, then, the picture be painted in seeming aloofness, or whether the novelist's self swoops on to and off the canvas, really doesn't matter much, for creative power and force of expression are the only real essentials.

The six great novelists whose profiles I

have so lightly sketched are all humanists. The foodstuff for their powers has in each case been gathered from the wayward currents of human feeling, the varying pulses of the human heart, the countless ironic realities of human existence. Whatever formal creeds (if any) they may have endorsed, their real creed is summed up in the dwarf's saying: "Something human is dearer to me than the wealth of all the world."

There is nothing of the literary popinjay in any of them; and they were not theorists, no—not even Tolstoi—theorists who would fit humanity to a scheme or art to a pattern. Human life was relative to them before Professor Einstein discovered relativity. I think they all believed that means justify ends. And though that may be only half the truth—like every proverb—it is the half suited to an age which has outworn dogma. Using the stuff of real life for the purposes of his art, a great novelist can, by the light he throws, forward the organic growth of human society, and colour the ethics of his time. He need not be conscious teacher or conscious rebel. He need only see widely, feel deeply, and be able to mould what he has seen or felt into that which has a new and significant life of its own. Did not the painter Manet say that the beginning of every new picture for him was like jumping into the sea without knowing how to swim? It is like that too for the novelist who pastures in the fields of human life. No patterns, no theories guide his efforts. He must discover. He must forge for himself out of life's raw material the design which suits.

Humanism is the creed of those who believe that, within the circle of the enwrapping mystery, men's fate is in their own hands, for better for worse; and these six novelists, by their natural absorption in all things human, and their great powers of expression, have furthered a faith which is becoming for modern man—perhaps—the only possible faith.

1924.

BOOKS AS AMBASSADORS

BOOKS AS AMBASSADORS

HAVE books done more to unite or to divide mankind? Have not the Bible, the Koran, and *Das Kapital*, notwithstanding their intentions, divided men more than all other books whatsoever have united them?

"I come not to bring peace but a sword" could be written with truth on the covers of a multitude of books, and the sentiment "Books as Ambassadors" must be qualified by as many saving clauses as an Act of Parliament.

We can acquit Euclid, and books on the condition of the moon, of making mischief; we can assert with safety that the works of Euripedes, Virgil, Petrarch, Shakespeare, Goethe, Montaigne, Cervantes, Dante have been positively unifying.

We may indeed go further and lay it down that any book which is a work of art and rouses impersonal emotion bears out this motto. Unhappily, much literature which has the quality of art is dreadfully diminished in translation. Poetry, and fiction with individual style, with flower of author in it, lose much when rendered out of their native garb. And these are just the books which most help to join the hearts of men, for they constantly remind us that within each Italian, each Pole, each Englishman, Russian, Frenchman, Austrian, Swede there is a human being who varies as little in essentials as bulldog from poodle-dog, whose life is the same tragicomedy, whose appetites, virtues and defects are neither more nor less appalling, and who, when his clock strikes, will pass through the same dark doorway.

Shakespeare's *Lear* and Balzac's *Père Goriot,* Tolstoi's *Anna* and Goethe's *Gretchen* bring the souls of readers to the same sweet waters. The same bright angels pass above us all when we hold our breath at the death of Bazarov, at the lovering of Romeo, at the divine madness of the immortal Don. When books are made in the large and welcoming spirit of Art they distil a balm into the parched human soul, and dispose it to gentilesse.

Dickens with his novels, Andersen with his fairy tales, a thousand and one other writers with their fancy folk have put a daub of cement between the bricks of human life, and traversed all national boundaries with every word they wrote. Far be it from this writer to decry or minimise the beneficent power of Literature when it can, even by some stretching of the imagination, be called Art. Than Art there is no greater mollifying force. None, indeed, so great. And we may go even further still and say that any book which, without exciting partisanship, hatred or contempt, familiarises us with what lies outside our normal experience will add to the pool of human unity by binding mind to mind with the cement of knowledge. *Encyclopedia Britannica,* the *Latin Grammar, Reading without Tears,* Vasari's *Lives of the Painters* and the *Child's Guide to Knowledge,* are impeccably on the credit side.

Thousands of harmonising books—Yes. But do they pull the balance down?

Ink is cheap, and man disposed to prejudice, to restless curiosity, to wrath, and partisanship. He lets loose currents of ink beyond his ken or his control. Hourly comes a fellow with some sacred bee in his bonnet, writes its buzzing down, and sets men by the ears. *The Divine Comedy* counts little beside the treatise of a Treitschke, when nitro-glycerine has been paid for and is waiting to be used. Praise of the arch-disturber Napoleon may be bought at half a crown the ream. Jingoes, Chauvinists, Pan-Whatnots find willing publishers, a Press to pat their backs, and Publics with the ears, but not the sense, of Balaam's ass.

And books—so well intentioned—have a way of familiarising us with horrors till we feel quite cosy about them. We grow inured to the idea of perishing wholesale, town by town, from poison gas dropping like the gentle dew from heaven, with possibly more noise, but certainly less warning. Books tell us that this is the natural course of the human serial, and gradually we think: "Dear me! Very awkward, but I suppose it is. Why worry?" And when some bright logician, in a tome at 5s. net, asks: "What is the matter with poisoning water supplies or disseminating the germs of typhus? It's all of a piece with nitroglycerine," we very soon think: "Well, what is the matter with it, anyway? War is war!" So it goes. Of course such books might be burned at birth, but then—they're not. *The Little Flowers of St. Francis* might be put into the hands of Labour, instead of *Das Kapital*—but is it?

No! Books will be books! Peace-making or belligerent, like men.

And the schism-working books are all written by such admirable fellows, confident that they are doing God's work and opening the eyes of mortals. How can one remonstrate with the patriotic soldier, whose simple stare has never seen anything but the good of his own country, when he recommends that country to commit any frightfulness, so long as it is detrimental to the enemy? It would be unkind. The man does his best. He has his lights. Or how reconcile it with freedom of speech and liberty of subject to incarcerate the poet who hales his country over hill, over dale, thoro' brake thoro' briar, to glorious conquest? It isn't done. On the contrary. And the industrious, the self-sacrificing scientist, who works and writes in the faith that knowledge justifies all—how dash from his lips the chalice of that credulity? Above all, the visionary, single-minded soul, who sees his vision and naught else, for whom the world is well lost in flood and fury, if his creed prevail—have we the heart so to dilute his ink that it becomes illegible? Not so. He, like the earthquake, has his uses.

We must suffer these—we must suffer from them and their books.

"Books as ambassadors"—well, yes! But ambassadors, before now, have been known to put the fat in the fire!

1924.

FAITH OF A NOVELIST

FAITH OF A NOVELIST

TRUTH, to human beings, is the same just relation of part to whole as that without which a living thing will not function. And the task before creative writers is the presentation of visions with the implicit proportions of truth, and so coloured by the temperament of their seers as to have the essential novelty of living things —for no two living things are alike, nor any two ways of seeing them similar.

A work of fiction, then, should carry the hall-mark of its author so surely as a Goya, a Daumier, a Velasquez, and a Mathew Maris are, as a rule, the unmistakable creations of those masters. This is not to speak of the tricks and manners that attract that facile elf the caricaturist, nor to imply that a novel should be a sort of sandwich, in which the author's mood or philosophy is the slice of ham. It is, rather, a demand for a subtle impregnation of flavour; an individual way of seeing and feeling such as, for instance, makes de Maupassant a more poignant and fascinating writer than his master Flaubert, and Dickens more living and permanent than George Eliot.

Some hold that the artist's sole function is the impersonal elucidation of the truths of Nature. But for the purposes of Art there are no such things as truths of Nature, apart from the individual vision of the artist. Seer and thing seen, inextricably involved one with the other, form the texture of any masterpiece. And such subtle intermingling of seer with thing seen is the outcome only of long and intricate brooding, a process not too favoured by modern life, yet without which we achieve little but a fluent chaos of clever insignificant impressions, a kind of glorified journalism.

The temperament of any considerable novelist is not likely to be a simple equation. The emotional and critical sides of his nature will be ever fighting a duel, first one then the other getting the upper hand,

and too seldom fusing into the balance of a drawn battle. And, according as the tides sway, so will be the effect on the reader. A novelist must ever wish to discover a member of the Public who, never yet having read a word of his writing, would submit to the ordeal of reading him straight through. Probably the effect could only be judged through an autopsy; but in the remote case of survival it would be profoundly interesting to the novelist to see the difference, if any, produced in his reader's outlook over life. Since there is a limit to human complaisance, he may never know the exact measure of his infecting power; or whether, indeed, he is not just a long soporific.

But no novelist who believes in giving value to his temperament will be always soporific. That which gets on his nerves will surely out, and more especially when his theme deals with the honeycomb we call Society. To think that birth, property, position, worldly superiority, in sum, is anything but a piece of good luck may be out of date, but Society takes itself for granted very subtly, and there is still little of a genuine "There, but for the grace of God, go I!" feeling in those who do not have to slave, struggle, and cadge for their livings; little power of seeing themselves as they might so easily have been but for their good fortune, little of the ironic eye, turned in as well as out. Quite modest and unassuming specimens in the upper sections of the honeycomb accept quietly, blindly, blandly, themselves, their clothes, habits, accent, manners, morals. This very deep, unconscious Pharisaism is to be found fitting like a skin on aristocrats professing the most democratic sentiments, on pastors proclaiming the most Christian doctrines, on intellectuals redolent of culture —so natural is it, so almost physical, so closely connected with the nerves of nose, and eyes, and ears.

The inevitable tendency, then, of the novelist who deals with social types, if he sees things in due proportion, will be to skin the knuckles of privilege.

FAITH OF A NOVELIST

A saying that used to be met with in almost every review of a novel was this: "The part of the artist is to see life steadily and to see it whole." It was generally used when a writer did not see life as his critic saw it, or when he implied that there was anything rotten in the state of Denmark. But "to see life steadily and to see it whole" is certainly not to see it with the eye of an established order, self-contented and contained. A section of life seen without relation to the rest of life has no perspective; is flat like a pancake. And such flatness in presentment is characteristic of the second-rate novelist. Another saying that used to be met with on the same page was this, "A work of art should be a criticism of life," which means nothing if not that an artist should see life with his individual or temperamental eye. It may be his misfortune, but is hardly his fault, if that eye does not take a complacent view of existence.

That those incompatibles Control and Freedom are both such excellent ideas is one of the profound ironies of life. Socialist and Tory, Liberal and Anarchist—both have good cases on paper; and yet the human being in us all is continually tearing them up and filling with them the waste-paper basket. The ills and irregularities of human society seem centred in defects which belong to us irrespective of privilege, party, or politics, and one would as soon expect them to be removed by Socialism, Bolshevism, Fascism, and so forth, as to see fulfilment of the gospel according to Mr. Stone in the novel *Fraternity!* That visionary's thin voice preaching to the night across a shadowy garden is no more the echo of possibility than are the dreams of controlled perfection in the human state. At best, we can but expect ebbings of the tides of inequality, with floods again to follow. This is the height of discouragement if social equality be considered an end in itself. But human happiness is the real end, and equality a somewhat glib and posturing means thereto.

In any case the novelist, if he is an artist, is neither politician nor schoolmaster; he can claim no teacher's temperament and no direct function. His contribution (not inconsiderable) to social and ethical values must be by way of the painting of character and environment. And such painting may take either of two forms—the negative, realistic and quasi-satiric, which stares Character straight in the face, or looks a little down at it, showing what men might be by giving defects due prominence; or the romantic, which stares up at Character, and shows what men might be by painting heroes or earthly paradises, and stressing their virtues and delights. A novelist, like his reader, is disposed by nature to one of these methods or to the other—occasionally to both.

To one who speaks with the partiality of a practitioner, the first method seems the most natural and effective. Most of the great characters of fiction, nearly all those who have contributed to ethical values—Don Quixote, Sancho Panza, Hamlet, Lear, Falstaff, Tom Jones, Faust, d'Artagnan, Sam Weller, Betsy Trotwood, Micawber,

Becky Sharp, Major Pendennis, Bel-Ami, Irena, Bazarov, Natasha, Stepan Arcadyevitch, Anna Karenina—have been conceived and painted in that manner. The sophisticated reader does not like being led by the nose, any more than the sophisticated novelist—so far as one may speak for that breed—likes leading him. The intelligent prefer to deduce for themselves rather than to be shown the shining example; for, however it may be in life, in fiction the heroic cloys the palate. We find a clear if crude illustration of that truth in the figure of Athos in Dumas's Musketeer series. In the first part, when he is not fighting he is usually drunk, and we love him. In the second and third parts he has become so noble that the tortuous Aramis, the portentous Porthos usurp his place in our affections. The demand for the perfect or heroic in fiction is, indeed, the cry of such as do not understand the implications of their own request. It is a sure sign of inexperience; and, in general, evidence of a deficient æsthetic sense.

The novelist, then, if he deal with Society, and has anything of the critic in him, will unconsciously be something of a satirist. Telling the truth, as he sees and feels it, he will not subscribe to popular superstitions, however wholesome; and when he is painting Society he cannot avoid treading on corns or holding foibles up to daylight. To him each section of Society, professionals and plutocrats, squirearchy, intellectuals, aristocrats—each will have its weak point, its doom; the negative, so to speak, of its virtues. To illustrate from one's own work: The Forsytes, with all their sound and saving sense, have their exaggerated love of property; the Pendyces of *The Country House* in their pluck a core of crass obstinacy; the Dallisons of *Fraternity*, to their cultured sympathy the appendix of fastidious indecision; and the Carádocs of *The Patrician*, though endowed with the sense of duty, decisiveness, and high spirit, are atrophied in their emotional capacity by their inbred love of leadership. But though it is the novelist's part to hold up a mirror so that people see themselves as they are, we may trust the Forsytes, Pendyces, and Carádocs of this life to remain unaware of their special "dooms"; and to carry on, lifting their noses above the satirist and all his works, while the intellectual Dallisons will already have seen their doom before it is shown to them.

What purpose then will the novelist serve? Well! By depicting a section of life in due relation to the whole of life without fear or favour, he does not cure the section, but he does throw it into proper relief for the general eye, and indirectly fosters evolution.

If, on the other hand, his theme is more elemental and he is treating, say, of passion, he can but ill speak truth, walking with his right hand in Mrs. Grundy's and his left hand in Dr. Watts'! And yet to write grossly of sex, to labour in a story the physical side of love is to err æsthetically—to over-paint; for the imagination of readers requires little stimulus in this direction, and the sex impulse is so strong that any emphatic physical description pulls the picture out of perspective. A naive or fanatical novelist may think that by thoroughly exploring sex he can reform the human attitude to it; but a man might as well enter the bowels of the earth with the intention of coming out on the other side. If it were not for the physical side of love we should none of us be here, and the least sophisticated of us knows intuitively so much about it that to tell us more, except in scientific treatises, is to carry coals to Newcastle. But the atmosphere and psychology of passion are other matters; and the trackless maze in which the average reader wanders where his feelings are concerned is none the worse for a night-light or two. In every artist, moreover, who is not a freak there is a sensibility to the scent and colour of the Dark Flower, to its fascination, and the fates lurking within its lure, which demands a vent. And though—especially in England and America—many novelists deliberately stifle this sensibility, and treat of passion exclusively as the prelude to wedding-bells, they do so at the expense of truth and their stature as artists.

The school of thought which would limit a novelist's range of subject to what may desirably be placed in the hands of the young person has been summed up in the figure of Podsnap, and is of course primarily Anglo-American. But whatever explanation biologists may offer of the puritanical streak in Anglo-Saxon blood will leave the artist unconsoled and open to the attacks of a particularly virulent type of intolerance, which in turn produces a spirit of revolt, often expressing itself in terms of sexual exaggeration equally undesirable. The artist is better advised to pay no attention, but to tell the truth as delicately and decently as he can. *L'excès est toujours un mal,* whether in Puritan or his victim.

The artist, they say, is not concerned with morals, but in truth no one is more concerned with morals if a long view be taken. For to the artist we look for those pictures of life as it really is, those correlations of sectional life to the whole, essential to the organic moral growth of human society. Moralists, preachers, judges, business men are all by nature or occupation advocates of the *status quo;* radicals and reformers are all professional partisans of the millennium. But history tells us that the *status quo* is of all things most liable to depart, the millennium of all things least likely to arrive; and the artist, alone steering clear of *parti pris,* furnishes the light by which the path of—if not progress—at least development can be discerned.

Conversion of others to his own way of thinking, however, is certainly no direct part of a novelist's business. Let him think and let think. When he has so selected and arranged his material as to drive home the essential significance of his theme, and pressed out from human nature the last ounce of its resistance to Fate, he has done his job; but in so doing he may often seem to be exploiting some social problem, or grinding the axe of a reform, when he has really only selected circumstances and environment which will most surely and suitably bring out the fundamental qualities of his characters.

The emotional, social, or political extravagances of society pass the skill of doctors, and their redress must be left to Nature, who—generally at the eleventh hour—administers a purge so drastic that it kills or cures. The world has an incurable habit of going on, with possibly a tendency towards improvement in human life; and the novelist, like any other specimen of mankind, fits into the slow pattern, and cannot flatter himself that he is directly altering the regulator or accelerating the pulses of the clock. His influence, sometimes a very real if subtle influence, is confined to a mental quickening, to a species of spiritual infection from his positively or negatively expressed passion. All he can do is to present truth as he sees it, and, gripping with it his readers, produce in them a sort of mental and moral ferment, whereby vision may be encouraged, imagination enlivened, and understanding promoted. And always he must expect to be mistaken and to be criticised.

Of art as a whole it is safe to say that the critic should always be ready to accept the theme and the medium selected by the artist, and having accepted, should then criticise the work for being, or not being, what it is meant to be. But this counsel of perfection is not often followed even by critics who would admit its truth. In going our own ways we novelists will be charged with many opposite faults of temperament and texture, and if we are impressionable will stop writing out of sheer bewilderment. We shall be rated for pessimism and for idealism; for soulless impartiality and for sentimentality; for chilly artistry and for rash propagandism; for barren cleverness and for naive humanitarianism; for bitterness and for sweetness; for lack of vision and for being visionary; and often, perhaps, with justice. But the fact is that a self-consciousness which checks or heats our moods in response to criticism reduces us to impotence. Better that we take ourselves as the tides of our being dictate, and let ourselves go upon them; for, after all, we do not choose our subjects—it is they who choose us. Life forces itself on us and gives us no rest until it has secured expression and received thereby quietus. But in going our own ways let it be *æquo animo*, laying no flattering unction to our souls.

The beauty of the world is the novelist's real despair; the heartache that he feels in the presence of Nature in flower. Maybe that ache is part of the sex instinct—a longing for fusion or union with beauty beheld; or, more rudely, might be called greed—the desire for the perpetual and intimate possession of loveliness. The effort to paint or render that loveliness in words is, then, a natural resort, an attempt to slake longing, which achieves, alas! but the mere shadow of fulfilment.

Truth and beauty are a hard quest, but what else is there worth seeking? Absorption in that quest brings to the novelist his reward—unconsciousness of self, and the feeling that he plays his part as best he may. At the back of all work, even a novelist's, lies some sort of philosophy. And if this novelist may for a moment let fall the veil from the face of his own, he will confess: That human realisation of a First Cause is to him inconceivable. He is left to acceptance of what is. Out of Mystery we came, into Mystery return. Life and death, ebb and flow, day and night, world without beginning and without end is all that he can grasp. But in such little certainty he sees no cause for gloom. Life for those who still have vital instinct in them is good enough in itself, even if it lead to nothing further; and we humans have only ourselves to blame if we alone, among the animals, so live that we lose the love of life for itself. And as for the parts we play, courage and kindness seem the elemental virtues, for between them they include all that is real in any of the others, alone make human life worth while and bring an inner happiness.

1926.